The Battle Bulge
A Memoir

By
Sheldon Zerden

Table of Contents

1. Dedication
2. About the Author
3. Introduction
4. Why This Book was Written
5. The Forgotten Slaughter
6. A Fearless Leader
7. A Snapshot of the Battle of the Bulge
8. Pictures and Maps
9. Into the Maelstrom
10. When it all Started
11. The Roaring Twenties
12. What it was Like
13. The Early Years
14. Moore Street
15. The Candy Store
16. The 2 Cents Plain
17. My First Brooklyn Dodger Baseball Game
18. The Stillwell Theatre
19. Coney Island
20. The Balloon Tire Bike
21. The Accordion Fascination
22. Lafayette High School
23. The Day That Will Live in Infamy
24. Brooklyn College

25. Photo Gallery

26. Fort Dix
27. Carolina in the Morning
28. Basic Training
29. Over There
30. On the Beach
31. The 2,000 Plane air Raid
32. The Paris Escapade

33. A new Life Amid the Dying
34. A Belgian Interlude
35. The Malmedy Massacre
36. Frostbite
37. The 12th General Hospital in England
38. A Kosher Meal
39. Victory in Europe
40. Non-Fraternization
41. My Occupation Duties
42. The Kitchen Accident
43. How to Build a Dance Hall
44. Drying up Hoy
45. The German Funeral
46. The U.S.O. Troupe
47. Almost Raped
48. General's Mess
49. A Major Throat Cure
50. Frankfurt Synagogue on Passover
51. A Furlough to Paris
52. My Nuremberg Trial
53. The Purple Heart Ceremony
54. A Beer in Kassel
55. General Patton's Fatal Accident
56. Munich: Where it all Started
57. The Final U.S.O. Show
58. The Train to Camp Lucky Strike
59. A sad Farewell
60. Epilogue

To Daniel, Benjamin, and Sarah

About the Author

Sheldon Zerden is an award-winning author of seven books. His "Best Books on the Stock Market" was selected as the book of the year in finance by the American Library Association. For the last two decades, he has devoted his efforts to medical research, which gave rise to "The Best of Health: The 100 Best Health Books" and "The Cholesterol Hoax." His writing combines the analytical insight and thoroughness of a stock market strategist with a serious interest in health issues. The second edition of "The Best of Health" builds on the solid foundation of his past work and adds a score of outstanding books that highlight advances in alternative and integrative medicine.

"My War: A Memoir" is an actual account of Sheldon Zerden's war experiences with the legendary First Infantry Division, The Big Red One. His Combat Medic Badge, Purple Heart, and Bronze Star were earned in addition to four battle stars. His wounds resulted in a 90 day hospital stay in England, before returning to duty.

Introduction

What is the measure of your life? Is it the money you accumulate to leave your children? Or is it rather the contribution you make to your family, friends, community, and country. Everyone touches the people around him in many ways that he doesn't realize.
Remember George Bailey in the movie "It's a Wonderful Life." He was able to see what the world would be like if he had never been born. He made a major difference in the lives of so many people that he was a very important member of his community. He saved so many lives that the people in Bedford Falls gave all their hard-earned money to him when they thought he was in trouble. His family's cook gave him all the money "she was saving for a divorce, if she ever got married."

The point I'm making is that every person affects the people he meets as he journeys through life. I know I did. I have had an interesting story to tell, and for some reason I never sat down and wrote an account of my life. I have published seven books, but now is the time to tell my story. I can't wait. It's getting late. So many people have asked me about my experiences during the Battle of the Bulge as a combat medic with the legendary First Infantry Division (the Big Red One). I've finally decided to write my actual record of that time. It was the biggest battle of World War II. Thousands of Americans were killed and wounded.

This personal memoir is written by a person that has not gained the fame of celebrity. My personal feeling is that self-esteem is reward enough for my accomplishments. The Purple Heart, The Bronze Star, and the Combat Medic Badge are my Tony, Emmy, and Oscar.

My background will precede the story of a war that was fought long ago in a foreign land for a reason that I think has lost its meaning. The majority of the people who are alive today know nothing about the time, the purpose, or the importance of our commitment.

Sheldon Zerden,
Brooklyn, NY

Why This Book Was Written

I may be one of the only World War II veterans left who can write a book that tells the story of the Battle of the Bulge from personal, first-hand experience. I will revisit all the events that happened to me before I joined the First Infantry Division as a combat medic. I will try to recall my six months in Southern England, the landing in Normandy (D-Day + 20), the stay on the beach through August 1944, the traveling through France, running a dispensary in Liege, Belgium, and Joining the Big Red One after the Germans broke through before Christmas, 1944 in a desperate attempt to prevent the Allies from invading their "Fatherland."

The events are indelibly burned into my brain. They pour forth instantly. It is as though they happened yesterday. I haven't talked about my front line exploits at all for the last sixty-eight years. They are clear in my mind, although some of the names of the people are uncertain. I can see their faces as if they were in the room with me now.

Seven thousand World War II veterans die every week. There are still millions of men and women who fought in the war to end all wars. They are in their eighties and nineties, and soon they will be a memory, including yours truly. That is another reason why I am writing this record of the fight to save the world for democracy. It is eerie that we are once again fighting to preserve our way of life. This time we are at war with a faceless enemy; Muslim fanatics have hijacked a major religion that represents more than one billion people. They are ruthless and kill without remorse. They even kill Muslims who don't share their fundamentalist views.

I assure you that my journey will have some interesting vignettes that include meeting celebrities such as Joe Louis, President Eisenhower (then general in charge of all the Allies), Bing Crosby, Bob Hope and others. Come along for the ride.

The Forgotten Slaughter

From the beginning of World War II, until the present, the war's miseries have been described in all their agonizing details to the people of America. The horror our G.I's saw and the hardships they withstood have been extolled to the nation, and they did not fall on unsympathetic ears. The people of our country have always been sentimental, and they had a personal cause to feel moved by the misfortunes of war suffered by our own men. A true appreciation of the brutal realism of war leaves those excluded with fervent thanks that he was spared the necessity of seeing or experiencing the grim realities of war.

I saw war at first hand, and the things I observed are not pleasant to relate. It is true that I was forced to seek the warmth of an American Army Hospital in England after some time at the front, but this escape could not erase the bloody tangle of combat that remains clearly in my mind to this day. Men lived hand in hand with death every moment of the time they faced the enemy. Those who lived through the ordeal of war can well afford to laugh about it, for they have in reality cheated the angel of death—the same angel who caught up with so many of their buddies.

The average person tends to forget easily, but the abattoir that is war can still be remembered vividly by those who have experienced its horrors. Politicians and statesmen move people about like so many pawns. It would be well for them to recall the Hell that the last war was before they maneuver us into another one.

I served as a Combat medic with the 26th Infantry Regiment of the First Infantry Division. I was attached to a platoon in the first battalion. The time was a little after Christmas 1944. The German breakthrough had all but annihilated the green 99th and 106th Divisions, and the 1st, 2nd, 4th, and 9th Infantry Divisions were forced to return from a rest area somewhere in Belgium. The veterans of these fighting divisions were called back from a well-deserved rest to take up the fight once more with a desperate German offensive force. The snow was deep and the going was tough, but it wasn't the first time these fine outfits had to fight under miserable conditions. Everyone was equipped with a white snowsuit for camouflage purposes, and these cumbersome outfits made the fighting more difficult.

My division struck out at dawn on the 13th of January, 1945 to cut a vital road which connected Butgenbach with St.Vith. The surprise attack caught many Germans asleep in their shallow fox holes, and they were either shot or bayoneted. There were many other Germans who were not caught sleeping, and they fought savagely to protect their last stronghold before their own Siegfried Line.

I was at the forward aid station when the attack started, and I helped with the wounded. Men were brought in steadily with frozen feet, broken arms, shattered ankles, and disfigured faces. Little had been done to temper the ugly and brutal quality of their wounds, and it would not take too much imagination to compare that aid station with a slaughterhouse. When the attack had spent its fury, I was sent up to one of the platoons at the front. The moment that every soldier dreaded had come for me, and I fearfully set out to perform my duty as a medic, with my aid kit slung over my shoulder, and a prayer on my lips.

The terrifying feeling that a soldier has when he faces almost certain death can never be adequately described. It consumes his whole being with fear, and his nerves are as jumpy as hot grease in a frying pan. The dead are lying all around as sullen reminders of what could be in store for him. He thinks of home and of all the safe places he ever knew. The thoughts flash through his mind in quick time, and he finds himself on the field of combat with death at the next turn. These are the things I experienced as I cautiously dodged the enemy's missiles on my way to my new post.

Company C's command post was as busy as a New York night club. Telephone wires crowded the stairs that led down to the captain's room. Men were rushing back and forth and the wounded lined the floor. The command post was used as a clearinghouse for the wounded. Evacuation was hampered by the influx of new casualties, and the constant shelling of the enemy added to the confusion.

All I can now remember of my stay at the front is blood, death, and misery. People hate war because they know the toll it takes in unhappiness and suffering, and most people forget in times of emotion the inevitable result of war. It is with this in mind that I have written my story. Remember-nobody wins, chaos and economic upheaval reign after a war, a bitter sequel to the greater evil of wholesale human sacrifice.

A Fearless Leader

I had gained a very unfavorable impression of officers while serving in the Army. For more than two years I worked under officers who took advantage of their high position in the ranks and treated men like slaves. I did my work grudgingly because I had little respect for the leadership ability of my officers.

When the German armies broke through in the Ardennes (The Bulge), I was shipped west for infantry training. I was shuttled through several replacement depots until I found myself in the Medical Detachment of the 26th Infantry Regiment of the First Infantry Division, The Big Red One.

It was at the front lines that I first met Lt. John Kowalski. He was wearing a large, cumbersome snowsuit and he looked older than his thirty years. It was John who made me revise my opinion of army officers. He was so pleasant, helpful, and understanding that you had to like him. He lived in the same filth and under the same harrowing conditions that his men did. His calm and reassuring manner was a quality that was vitally necessary to keep green, inexperienced replacements from "blowing their top." After a few weeks had passed my liking for him developed into a deep, warm friendship. Since I was the "doc" I was in constant contact with him, and continually informed him of all the deaths and casualties. John took a fatherly interest in his boys and at times I saw him crying when we had lost a good man.

One night the platoon CP was buzzing, and the nervous youngsters were griping to the officers in charge. They said that the large corporations were the cause of the war and we were just fighting the war and risking our necks for them. John Kowalski spoke.

"Listen boys, you're not fighting for anyone but yourselves. You're fighting for your mothers, fathers, and all the kids you know. Those Nazis out in the woods thought they could rule the world, but we're here to prove that they can't rule us."

The German guns rumbled on and the boys moved their lips in silent prayer. I was thanking God that I had a leader as brave and unwavering as John, a man who could silence the fears of a bunch of youngsters even in the face of death. Some time later, I would be called out of the command post to patch up some G.I.s, and when I returned I saw two men on their backs. One of them was John. I held back a tear as I looked at him. His arm was perpendicular to his body and his forefinger was pointing to the heavens. Even in death this brave man told his men to have faith, to believe, to fight on. At that point, I would be a day away from being evacuated to the hospital, so I don't know who replaced John Kowalski. Whoever replaced him would have to be awfully good to instill the faith-born fighting spirit that Lt. John Kowalski did in the hearts of his men.

A Snapshot of the Battle of the Bulge

It was Hitler's last gamble. He sent two Panzer Armies into the Ardennes. The snow was waist deep. Kids and sick old men were all he had left. It was Christmas. It was truly a "scene for a Christmas card." Smooth white hills-dark forests-small villages nestled in the freezing, bitter cold. Our thunderbolts smashed the German staff cars. They lined the road to Bastogne. Half-tracks and tanks were mangled by direct hits from the bombs. Debris consisted of papers, tin cans, cartridge belts, a shoe, helmets, clothing, etc.

Frozen corpses of Germans, ignored and completely inhuman lay in the snow where they fell. The 101st Airborne Division still held Bastogne. They were entirely surrounded. They were constantly shelled and bombed. They fought off four times their number in Germans. Yet the survivors were cheerful and lively.

The American dead were moved inside the smashed houses and covered. The dead horses and cows lay where they were, just like the Germans. Down the street a command car dragged a trailer. The frozen bodies of Germans were piled on the trailer like so much ghastly firewood.

War is lonely, individual work. There were many dead and wounded, but the survivors turned the Germans back and into a retreat. This was not done fast or easily, and it was not done by those anonymous things like armies, divisions, and regiments. It was done by men, one by one, your men.

Men lived in their fox holes, one or two in a hole. No winter boots. Toes froze up to the size of softballs and turned black. If gangrene set in their toes had to be amputated. Men's overcoats became soaked with moisture and caked with mud and freezing rain.

Into the Maelstrom

"Just follow this road for about half a mile," said the sergeant, "C company is in that clump of trees."

I had just joined the First Infantry Division, (the Big Red One). I was in the 26th Regiment, Company C. I had chosen to be a combat medic rather than a rifleman. The captain gave me the opportunity to choose either one. I had been running a dispensary in the Belgian city of Liege, and had about three months of experience treating medical problems at sick call every morning. If I got into trouble I would call a doctor at the hospital.

The ground was covered with snow when we reached the assembly area of the First Division. Everyone was called up---mechanics, clerks, musicians, and me. The breakthrough by a desperate General Von Rundstedt's remnant of the once great German war machine was a big surprise. It caught our commanders napping. 250,000 Germans and 600 tanks swept through the American lines in the Ardennes forest causing massive panic and confusion. Thousands of soldiers, numb with fear, dropped their weapons and ran. They were like stampeding cattle. The untested 106th division gave up, hungry and sick. Von Rundstedt's breakthrough was "the most frightening, unbelievable experience of the war." Most American forces did not run, but stood their ground and held their positions. The biggest enemy was the bitter cold weather. A gruesome sight was seeing G.I.s sitting on the frozen bodies of the dead, before they were evacuated.

The commanding officer of our regiment assembled everyone on a flat, wide area behind the front lines. Hundreds of folding cots were set up in tents, where we slept with all our clothes and coats before joining our companies.

"We are the Big Red One, a fighting outfit. We have a history of being the first division called upon when trouble arises. We are in trouble now. That is why you are here."

He then drew a line in the snow with his combat boots, and said,

"Anyone who doesn't want to fight with the Big Red One, cross that line!"

No one did. We were all willing to fight with this legendary division. It was a privilege.

Three of us were assigned to Companies A, B, and C as combat medics. I remember the name of the medic for B Company. His name was Frost. When I arrived at the command post to report to the company commander it was hard to imagine how we could get anything done. The command post was busy, with wounded men on stretchers lying all over the place, telephone wires were everywhere. The traffic was heavy.

As I entered the post, they were carrying in a wounded soldier in a blanket. It was Frost. He was on the line for only an hour, and there he was with hundreds of shrapnel holes in his arms and legs. It was my introduction to the war at the front. I could just imagine what was going to happen to me when I got to my company.

I started up the road toward the trees where my company was dug in. We lived in foxholes deep enough to sit in and not have our heads sticking out above the lip of the hole. The Germans, on the other hand, just scooped out some soil, and crouched in to hide their body. Their holes were temporary. They obviously thought they would be moving forward, and didn't think they should spend the time to dig deep, permanent holes.

The ground was so hard it was like chipping away at concrete to dig a foxhole. I had no trouble, because all the men in my company wanted me to be with them, because "doc" would take care of them if they were wounded.

The snow-covered road was passable, but I was walking into an unknown future, fraught with danger. Artillery shells were sailing overhead, whistling their familiar song. I hit the ground several times, because I hadn't yet learned to judge whether the shells would land close to me or continue in their flight. I noticed a soldier walking toward me. As another artillery shell sounded close to us, we both hit the ground to escape the blast. We were only about ten feet apart, and as we arose and looked at each other, I recognized him.

"Adams—what the hell are you doing here?" I said

'Hey, Red, I'm in B Company up in that patch of trees," he replied.

Adams and I were in basic training together in the States, in North Carolina. I hadn't seen him in more than nine months. It was nice to see an old friend, but we had no time to chit chat. There was work to do and a war to be won. So Adams continued to walk toward the command post I had just left, while I continued to find my way to my new assignment, C Company, 26th Regiment of the famed First Infantry Division, the Big Red One. With trepidation, I walked toward the trees.

I was still unsure that I was headed in the right direction. I stopped short when I saw a clump of clothes lying in the road. Was it a direct hit by a mortar shell or artillery shell? My answer came shortly thereafter when I saw an arm lying in the road about thirty feet from the spot where the clothes were. It was scary. Further up the road I saw a soldier leaning against a tree with his rifle pointed straight out. At first I thought he was pointing it at me. But when I got closer, I saw it was an American. I thought I might ask him if he knew where my company was located. I know I was getting close. It was better to make sure that I knew where I was going.

"Hey, bud—do you know where C Company is located?" I said. No answer.

"Are you in the 26th Regiment," I asked

Silence.

I looked closer. This guy was dead. He was frozen into a Madam Tussaud-like figure leaning against the tree. The graves registration team hadn't cleared the field after the last attack. That was another experience that was not helping me to look forward to my job with joy.

I finally arrived at the Company C command post and checked in with Lieutenant Kowalski. He told me to buddy up with someone and take cover. There was constant shelling with mortars, artillery, and machine-gun fire. Shrapnel was falling everywhere, and you could see the smoke coming out of the bits of shrapnel that landed near you. I did so immediately, and tried to find out what the story was. We were on a hill, sequestered in a grove of trees, overlooking a valley that stretched for about 200 yards. At the far end of the valley were the Germans, who were also on a hill covered with trees. I dug a foxhole all by myself and climbed into it to avoid the shelling.

It was no consolation to know that it was the end game for Hitler and his master race. He sent 10-year old kids and sick old men into battle to save his precious Third Reich, "The Fatherland." It was cold, maybe 10 degrees below zero. While the machine pistol bullets were shattering the air with their annoying staccato, and the devastating 88 artillery shells were landing close by, all we could think of was how to keep warm. It was impossible. Yes, staying in the foxhole was important to avoid getting hit, or sliced apart by shrapnel, but direct hits by mortar shells took their toll. The Germans had us zeroed in. They poured an enormous amount of stuff at us. It was constant, and annoying, if not frightening.

When I returned to my foxhole after patching up some wounded soldiers, there were several bodies lying face up alongside their holes. Not a scratch on them, a peaceful look on their faces. The concussion of a direct hit causes the brain to swell or expand in the skull and it results in instantaneous death. Thoughts rushed through my head. Can anything be worse than a nineteen year old boy losing the chance to live a life, to get married, have a family, a dream, a future? They never had a chance, I thought, as I crawled, face down, toward my foxhole. As I passed the other foxholes, the boys looked up and asked me who was wounded, how bad was it? It was odd. Here we were, all replacements and we didn't even know each others' names. There really wasn't time to get to know the fellows around you. The turnover was so high, that no sooner did you become friendly with a neighbor, he was gone. He was either killed or wounded. After one sustained attack our company of 200 men was left with only 40. The Germans still had plenty of fight left in them. The ranks of the men in C Company had dwindled so much that a new replacement was elevated to company commander only three days after he joined us. He received a "battlefield commission."

A couple of weeks after joining the company, I was sitting in the command center with the company commander and exchanging information about the wounded and the dead. We heard a cry.

"Medic! Medic!"

"Hey, doc, they're calling you," said the lieutenant.

"Do I have to go out there now? I said. "A guy could get killed out there."

"I know," said the lieutenant," but that's your job!"

I crawled through the snow drifts, with machine guns and 88 artillery shells raking the area I was traversing. I kept my head down, eating snow, as I gradually made my way to the wounded soldier. I never wore a red cross on my helmet or on my arm. It made too good a target. It must have been 400 or 500 feet before I reached him.

When I surveyed the scene before me, my heart sank. The soldier was a signal corpsman who was stringing wire on a telephone pole. An 88 artillery shell sliced through the pole and severed both legs at the thigh. I was unusually calm considering what I had just seen. I thought to myself, maybe it was fruitless to try and save him. Blood was oozing out of every artery and vein in his legs. I could see a cross section of each thigh—bones, blood vessels, etc. He must have been in shock, but he was conscious, and he said, pleadingly,

"Save me, doc!"

I worked as fast as I could. Time was crucial. He had lost most of his blood. I had only one tourniquet. I put it around one stump. I quickly took my belt and applied it to the other stump. Then I emptied my sulfa powder on hundreds of tiny shrapnel holes all over his body and on the face of his two stumps. The bleeding stopped immediately, and I yelled out loud for the stretcher bearers. German prisoners were carrying our wounded off the field.

"Schnell Schweinhundt!" I shouted.

Speed was important. They had to carry the wounded man back to the forward aid station. We lifted him on to the stretcher, and put his severed legs on as well. I wished him good luck, and he smiled weakly. Off they went. They carried him away to an unknown future. I did follow up the case, and I found to my satisfaction that he did survive, and was in good shape in the hospital. But, was I in good shape? What about my future? I was still here, in the cold, facing an uncertain fate.

As I crawled back to my foxhole, I realized that the weeks of taking care of the wounded had taken their toll. Sleep was impossible, it was too cold. The food was not enough to nourish you at the optimal level. You had to subsist on K rations and occasionally a truck came by with hot soup and a carton of cigarettes. Again, the boys in all the foxholes were curious about who was hit and how serious was the wound.

I reached my foxhole, and dragged my frozen, weary body into its relative safety before the darkness of the cold, windy, Ardennes forest descended on the area. I immediately fell into a deep sleep that transported me far away from my current dilemma.

When it all Started

Late in the 19th Century, a wave of immigration from Eastern Europe—Russia, Poland, Romania, etc. brought hundreds of thousands of the oppressed peoples of the old world to the promise of a new life in America. The freedom to work hard and forge a new life for your family was enough incentive for these people to leave everything they had behind, and find their way to the best country in the world.

It was not easy for my ancestors to walk hundreds of miles, sleeping in strange places, barns, fields, and anywhere they could find shelter. There were pogroms in Czarist Russia that destroyed whole villages and shtetls. The Cossacks rode into their towns and burned, raped, and pillaged at will. Thousands of Jews were killed and maimed. My grandfather was president of the Berditchever Society, a fraternal order. In 1905 there was a pogrom in Berditchev. My mother lived in a little village called Christinovka and my father came from another shtetl close by called Monastrishte

They didn't meet until they came to America. When the Czar tried to conscript everyone into the Russian Army it was the last straw. My father and his brothers struck out for the border. They braved the elements, the unfriendly farmers, and the authorities in the cities, and the border guards. They finally arrived in the seaport cities of Germany. Separately, my father Max and his brother Benjamin made their way to New York and Ellis Island. When they were able to send money to the old country, they brought their mother Shayna (Sophie), their sisters Sarah (Buptzie) and Mollie, and their younger brother Samuel to America. Eventually the whole family came to America. My father's father Yehuda died when Max was thirteen. He succumbed to a burst appendix. Both of the villages where my parents lived were in Ukraine, then part of Czarist Russia, and were several kilometers from Kiev.

The same story was true of my mother's family. Her father Louis and mother Sarah, and all of the seven surviving children were eventually united on the East side of Manhattan, one of America's melting pots. There was no welfare, no food stamps, and no healthcare. You were on your own. My mother's family consisted of sisters Zlota, Rosie, Frieda, and Alice (my mother). The brothers were Samuel, Arthur, and Barney. The family name was Gellman.

Benjamin Zerden and Samuel Gellman, my two uncles, joined the United States Army and fought in France in World War I. That was the dues they paid to show their appreciation for the opportunity to live in this great country. Both of them were successful businessmen who built companies from the ground up. They had no help. It took drive, passion, and persistence. They had to learn the language and build a business with difficulty. But they had no quit in them. It took Sam five or ten different jobs before he established his own machinery business in Centre Street in New York. He eventually invested in real estate and bought commercial buildings and apartment houses. He started with no money, no contacts, nothing but the drive, the ambition, the character, and the honesty to forge a life for himself and his family. His wife was Olga and my four cousins were Norman, Miriam, Sheldon, and Richard. It was truly an American success story. I loved my Uncle Sam. He was the real thing.

My Uncle Ben was also successful as a manufacturer of ladies' apparel. He started as a partner with my father, Max, at his shop in Brooklyn, and moved to New Jersey to establish a non-union shop. He bought the building which housed his factory and lived a comfortable life in New Jersey. His wife's name was Sarah, and my cousins were Edward and Ruth.

The Roaring Twenties

I was born at an exciting time in the history of America. The 1920s are called "roaring" because there were many things happening at the same time. Prohibition was the law of the land, but that many people ignored that law. It gave rise to speakeasies, where drinking and gambling flourished. American heroes were born and worshipped during this era. Charles Lindbergh flew to Europe in the "Spirit of St. Louis." It was a single engine monoplane. He was the toast of the United States and celebrated in Paris, where he landed. Babe Ruth was truly an inspiring story. He was called, "The Great Bambino" and "The Sultan of Swat, take your choice. He hit 60 home runs in one season when baseball used a "dead ball." He rocketed to fame and the Yankee Stadium was called, "The House That Ruth Built." His stature has grown through the years, and he is preeminent in the baseball world.

In the business world, the 1920s witnessed exponential growth of several industries. Automobile production for General Motors doubled every year in the early twenties. The advertising field was just beginning to find a growing market needed to justify its existence and claims. A whole new communications industry developed with radio. America was tuned in to "the Shadow," "the Lone Ranger," "Eddie Cantor," "Edgar Bergen and Charlie McCarthy," "Jack Benny," and a great many others. President Franklin Delano Roosevelt grew to popularity with his fireside chats on the radio. Radio Corporation of America RCA) and many other companies were selling Victrolas and the records that people wanted to play over and over again

Hollywood and the movie industry was in its infancy. Soon after the first talking picture that Al Jolson made, "The Jazz Singer," the movies came into their own, and in 1927, we had the first Academy awards. What an outstanding period! It all came crashing down in October, 1929 when the stock market made paupers out of millionaires overnight. The joke was going around at the time. A man was checking into a hotel, and the desk clerk asked,

" Sleeping or jumping?"

It was no joke for the many millions of unemployed who were standing on the street corner selling apples.

What it was Like

It seems like 100 years ago. In truth, it was almost that much. It was another world. You could hardly imagine how different life was for a person growing up during the depression years of the 1930s.

Can any kid today appreciate the convenience of a refrigerator? I grew up with an ice box. When the ice melted I had to get up in the middle of the night and empty the bowl or "schissel" under the ice box when it was filled with water. If I didn't wake up on time, the water that had melted from the ice would overflow the bowl and cause a flood in the kitchen.

That is only an introduction to the relatively primitive life of the thirties. Most homes did not have a telephone. Think of it! Every ten-year old boy and girl in school today has a cell phone. They can't even imagine life without being connected. No phone? How could anyone live like that? Well, if we got a call, the candy store on the corner received it on a pay phone, and some kid would run to the house and call us to the phone. He would get a couple of cents for a tip.

That seems like a paltry sum. But in those days a candy store had over 100 different kinds of candy for only one penny. We could stand in front of the showcase and select from a wide variety of candy treats. If we chose, we could play the pinball machine for a penny. People who smoked cigarettes could buy a pack of butts for about 14 cents. If you wanted to buy them loose a cigarette cost one cent. We didn't know that cigarettes were unhealthy. Lucky Strike, Chesterfield, Old Gold, Herbert Tareyton, Pall Mall, Helmar, Camels, Raleigh, Philip Morris, were some of the standard brands of cigarettes that were sold in the early thirties.

Bernie the barber charged my mother 25 cents for our haircuts. He was the source of all the news in the neighborhood. He knew everybody, and he was a fountain of information. He could tell you who was sick, who died, who moved, and he was not bashful about telling his patrons all the dirt. It was gossip central. The only other store on Bath Avenue between Bay 37th and Bay 38th Streets was Pop Costa's pool room. It was a hangout for all the guys. We all spent many nights in there.

All you needed was a nickel to buy a Mello-roll. It was a cylindrical-shaped ice cream cone. It was creamy and delicious. In the summer I would ask my mother for a nickel and buy a Mello-roll in Marlis' drug store. It was on the corner of Bath Avenue and Bay 37th Street. Every Tuesday night there was a fireworks display in Coney Island. We could see it very clearly from my corner. I wasn't alone. The whole block was there to enjoy the show.

I was ambitious and enterprising. I put in some time working in the drug store opening the many boxes of chemicals and drugs that Mr. Marlis used to mix and create his medicines. For a short time I worked at Cohen's grocery store delivering rolls and milk. He had a wagon filled with orders for his customers. Rolls cost 2 cents, and a quart of milk was 8 cents. The job didn't last too long. An eleven-year old kid had to get up at 7 o'clock in the morning and help fill the orders. Our rolls and bread were bought from Schlom and Deutsch bakery on Bay Parkway and 86th Street. Bread was freshly baked and so were the rolls and cake.

The Early Years

There was no epidemic of obesity in the early 1930s. People today spend too much time watching television, playing video games on their computers, and living a sedentary lifestyle. My youth was more active and allowed for a healthy mix of active sporting games, and a diet of wholesome nutritious foods. The following list of activities allowed my friends and I to enjoy our leisure time doing interesting things. Of course, there were no television sets and no computers to coax us into a sedentary, couch- potato lifestyle.

Kick the can, catty and stick, Johnny-on-the Pony, roller skating, roller hockey, football, softball, handball, boxball, stickball, stoopball, ring-a-leevio, chase the white horse, territory, Skelly, touch football, marbles, yo-yo, hide and seek, nuts in a hole, doctor, pick- up-sticks, monopoly, battleship, soccer, Punch-ball, post office, pin the tail on the donkey, spin the bottle, double Dutch, hopscotch, scooters, three wheelers, bicycles, badminton, volleyball, baseball, checkers, chess, casino, poker, rummy, 7 1/2 , 7 card stud, coin toss against the wall, baseball card collecting, coin collecting, stamp collecting, and tag.

The above list is just about all the activities, games, and leisure time pursuits that my friends and I enjoyed. We had no money. We didn't care. We didn't know the difference because we never had any. There wasn't a problem with obesity but a few of my friends were large. Ralphie Parness was a big guy, and we needed him for our football team.

Moore Street

My grandfather was born in 1860. Two of his brothers were killed in the Russo-Turkish War. Louis "Leb" Gellman made his way to America with the great wave of immigration from Eastern Europe. The immigrants who arrived in the new world were seeking religious tolerance and economic opportunity. My grandfather had seven children and a wife to support, and little time for creature comforts. His life was devoted to his shul (synagogue) and to his business. He had almost no education. He couldn't read or write English, but he had the ambition and drive to provide for his family. He bought a license to own and operate a pushcart on the bustling business street in Williamsburg, Brooklyn. Behind his modest enterprise was a storefront with a kitchen and a toilet. This kitchen had a table and a bare bulb electric light. It was at this same table that my uncle Barney studied and earned a scholarship to the Massachusetts Institute of Technology (MIT). His genes were obviously inherited by his son David Gillman, who was the youngest person to be invited to the Advanced Studies Institute at Princeton at the age of 22. He later was Assistant Dean of the Mathematics Department at the University of California at Berkeley.

Close to my grandfather's storefront was a small grocery store owned by the Waldbaum family. This area spawned many entrepreneurs. It was a shopping center that attracted hundreds of housewives in search of low prices for their fruits, vegetables, clothing, and other items. I was only 5 or 6 years old when I made my first visit to my grandfather's pushcart. I remember it vividly. Every market day my uncles Barney, Arthur, and Samuel would join their father, Louis, and load the pushcart with the best bargains they could find. When they returned to Moore Street, they unloaded their purchases in the store and packed the pushcart with fruits and vegetables for the day's business.

When I arrived at the street, I saw my grandfather sitting on a chair alongside his cart. The place was buzzing with activity. Louis Gellman had a brown paper bag filled with pennies, nickels, dimes, and quarters. I was struck with the fact that every item on his pushcart was selling for a penny a pound: Onions, potatoes, carrots, cabbage, squash, sweet potatoes, lettuce, cucumbers, and other vegetables. Fruits may have cost a couple of pennies more. I couldn't understand the significance of that visit. I was too young. However, I know now that the depression which America experienced was a bitter reality on the streets of Brooklyn. The picture of my mother's father selling potatoes for a penny a pound is burned into my memory; the humble beginnings of my family in America.

The Candy Store

What could be more exciting for an eight year old kid with 3 cents in his pocket than a visit to the corner candy store. Schwartz's candy store on Bath Avenue and Bay 37th Street was a hangout for all the young children in the neighborhood. The store was the center for the telephone, the pinball machine, and the giant showcase that had a great variety of penny and nickel candy. The following list of treats are some that I remember:

Bazooka Bubble Gum, Juicy Fruits, Jujubes, Nonpareils, Goobers, Black Crows, Good and Plenty, Mary Jane, Kerr's Butterscotch, Raisinets, Whoppers Malted Milk Balls, Chunkys, Horton's Chocolate Bars, Butterfingers, Oh Henry's, Sugar Dots, Life Savers, Wrigley's Gum, Twizzlers, Goldenberg's Peanut Chews, Topp's Baseball Cards, Milk Duds, York Chocolate Covered Mints, Milky Ways, Forever Young, Peter Paul's Almond Joys, Jelly Beans, Tootsie Rolls, Baby Ruth's, and Hershey's Mr. Goodbar. I am sure that you can remember other names that have survived more than 100 years like Cella's Chocolate Covered Cherries and Joyva Halvah. It was part of growing up. I loved it, and I wouldn't have missed it for the world. Most of today's boys and girls will never know the joys that I derived as a youth in that candy store. The fact is that many kids don't have a corner candy store. They can't walk down the block and meet their friends to play the pinball machine. In many places you need a car to get to the mall or buy a newspaper. The world I grew up in was very different from what many experience today.

The 2 Cents Plain

The whole depression of the 1930s could be defined by the 2 cents plain. A plain glass of seltzer or carbonated water cost only 2 cents at any soda fountain. You could, in fact, get a small glass for one cent. We used to ask the soda jerk to "sweeten it up" with some syrup. He usually obliged. If it was too sweet, he would put more seltzer in the glass.

Those days are gone. No more egg creams, no more 2 cents plains. I asked a soda jerk in a candy store how much it cost for a 2 cents plain, and he answered, without batting an eye,

"Eighty cents!"

So you can see how the value of the dollar has eroded through the years. When I was 12 years old, I would bring my lunch to school in a brown paper bag, and at J.H.S. 128 on 84th Street and 21st avenue in the Bensonhurst section of Brooklyn, I left the school for lunch. My friends and I ate in Maltz's Candy Store. It was across the street from the school. I could order a malted milk. Three glasses of malted with a long pretzel cost 12 cents. It was delicious because Maltz used a large scoop of ice cream and milk that was whipped up in a Hamilton Beach Malted Machine.

If you were hungry on the way home from school, you could buy a slice of pizza for a dime, or have a large cup of spumoni for 3 cents. The subway train cost only a nickel and you could ride all the way from Coney Island to the Bronx. Vim and Davega were two competing sporting goods stores, and a pair of sneakers cost about one dollar and twenty-five cents.

All through my childhood years I wasn't aware of money. I didn't have any and I really didn't need too much of it. All my needs were taken care of by my mother. She was frugal and stretched the few dollars that were essential for taking care of the family, her husband and three growing children. She cleaned, she cooked, she baked, she sewed, and we lived through the hard times without noticing how difficult it was to make ends meet. It just proves that you can prevail, even during the most difficult circumstances.

My First Brooklyn Dodger Baseball Game

It was 1934. I was 9 ½ years old. My brothers and I were rabid Dodger fans. They hadn't won the pennant since 1920, but their fans loved them. Every year the Dodgers ended in 7th or 8th place (the cellar). The faithful always said, "Wait 'till next year." In 1934, Casey Stengel, "The Old Professor," was the manager. Some of the names on the team were Al Lopez, Frenchy Bordegaray, Tony Cuccinello, Sam Leslie, Babe Phelps, John Cooney, and Goody Rosen. Some of the players were brought in from teams in other leagues like Joe Vosmik from Cleveland, and Heine Manush from the Washington Senators. They were a team of old timers and castoffs from other teams. Dixie Walker was a clutch hitter who won many games. Some of the pitchers like Watson Clark, Posedell, Pressnell, and Luke "Hot Potato" Hamlin won their share of games, but it was plain to see that they were not going anywhere. However, that didn't diminish the devotion Brooklyn fans had for their team. Hilda Chester had a cowbell in the bleachers (which cost 55 cents), and the fans had a great time with her and that bell. At third base we had Cookie Lavagetto. A fan would blow up balloons and yell "Cookie" all during the game.

It was true that the Dodgers were known for their foul-ups on the field, like three players on third base, or Babe Herman getting hit on the head with a ball. But the fans in the stands were just as wacky. Colorful is a euphemistic way to describe what went on at Ebbets Field. Babe Herman hit .392 in 1932, but he lost the batting title to Chuck Klein of the Phillies who hit .398 (I think). This is the background as I approached the day I attended my first major league baseball game.

It was a rare day when both of my brothers went to a ball game together. They had their own circle of friends and usually went with their friends. Pittsburgh was playing Brooklyn, and I convinced them to take me. It was the first and last time the three of us did anything together. I wore white long duck pants. When we arrived at Ebbets Field Eugene and Bernie bought tickets to the grandstand, which cost $1.25. The man taking the tickets at the turnstile let me in free. I don't know why, and I didn't care. I was going to see my first game.

    We found our seats behind first base upstairs. There were many empty seats and my brothers decided to move higher up into the right field area. They might have thought that a foul ball hit into that spot would be easier to catch. I stayed put and had a lot of people around me. Although the game had no significance, it was exciting for me. Pittsburgh had the Waner brothers, Lloyd and Paul ("Little Poison and Big Poison"), who were Hall of Fame caliber. The great Honus Wagner was their third base coach. Pie Traynor played third base, and Arky Vaughan, who was later traded to the Dodgers, was a great hitter with a wide open stance at the plate. These are some of the things a boy of nine remembers. Watson Clark was pitching for Brooklyn.

    In the third inning a foul ball by a right-handed batter curled up into the stands. It was heading right toward me, but it was pretty high. I acted quickly and stood up on my seat. It was the right thing to do. The ball flew into my hands, and the stands erupted into a loud round of applause. Here was a kid who made a bare-handed catch of a ball. Maybe he should be down on the field, and in uniform. Everyone applauded, even my brothers. They didn't know that I had caught the ball. They were too far away to notice that it was me. I was thrilled for two reasons. Besides being proud of myself, I had a baseball, and in those days, a baseball was a ticket to free admission to another game. A few innings later, another ball came up into the stands. This time I just stood up and the ball came right into my hands. Two baseballs in one game! I was the toast of the grandstands. The crowd roared with delight. The game became incidental. I was elated. When my brothers came down to take me home, they were stunned to find out that the guy they were applauding was their little red-headed brother. All-in-all it was a very exciting experience. My first day at the ball park, the Brooklyn Dodgers, Casey Stengel, and Honus Wagner. Wow!

The Stillwell Theatre

The center of a family's entertainment during the early 1930s was the radio. The Stromberg-Carlson, Philco, Zenith, RCA, Admiral, etc. made elaborate consoles which the family could gather around and hear their favorite shows. During the day there were soap operas like Stella Dallas, Just Plain Bill, Fibber McGee and Molly, Amos and Andy, and the Goldbergs. On Sunday night there was a vast array of choices. Jack Benny, Eddie Cantor, Edgar Bergen and Charlie McCarthy, the Shadow, the Green Hornet, the Lone Ranger, and the Lux Radio Theatre were some of my favorite shows. Other personalities that could be heard were Fred Allen, Major Bowes Amateur Hour, Al Jolson, Jimmy Durante, and the dominant voice of Arthur Godfrey and his variety show. Many of these performers made the transition to television. Among them were Bing Crosby, Perry Como, Dean Martin, and others.

In addition to these entertaining shows, there were sports and news commentators. There was no lack of entertainment for the radio listener. President Franklin Delano Roosevelt was a great communicator and used the radio with his fireside chats to propel himself to four terms as president.

Moving pictures were becoming popular as a medium of entertainment. Silent films gave way to talkies with Al Jolson's "The Jazz Singer" in 1927. The years that followed gave rise to many stars. Black and white films were dominant through the early thirties, and then color took over. Some of the stars of the thirties that I remember were Wallace Beery, Gary Cooper, Cary Grant, Jackie Cooper, Slim Somerville, John Garfield, Tyrone Power, John Payne, Robert Taylor, Jack Oakie, Ned Sparks, Jimmy Stewart, Clark Gable, Spencer Tracy, Katherine Hepburn, Mickey Rooney, and many others. Cowboy heroes were abundant. I enjoyed Westerns with Tom Mix, Jack Holt, William "Hop-along- Cassidy Boyd, Hoot Gibson, Ken Maynard, John Wayne, Gabby Hayes, Barton McLane, Roy Rogers, and many more.

The cost of admission to the movies was 11 cents. It was 10 cents and a penny tax. Tuesday night was "Ladies Night." They gave every lady a dish free when she came in on Tuesday. You could save up a whole set of china. I loved going to the Stillwell Theatre on 86th Street and 24th Avenue. If I didn't have a dime, I could turn in 5 Coke bottles and get 2 cents apiece. Every Saturday they had two main features, a cartoon, and a serial. It was a Western shoot-them-up. Each one ended with the cowboy about to go over a cliff with his trusty horse. The next week they show you how he jumps over the cliff to safety on the other side of the canyon.

It was a phase of my life that now seems benign. However, they were hard times. My friends were going through them also. Many people were out of work. There were no jobs. I remember my brother's friend Milton Siegel saying,

"Your cat Tiger eats better than I do!"

Coney Island

Long before Walt Disney opened his theme parks, the world's best play land was Coney Island. There was Luna Park and Steeplechase. You could spend a day at Luna Park where they had rides like the Submarine, the Dragon's Gorge, a Burlesque Show, a man shot out of the cannon, and many others. Each event cost only a nickel. Steeplechase was even more exciting. You could buy a ticket for all the rides for fifty cents and if you chose one, they punched the ticket for that number. Steeplechase had the Barrel of Fun, and the world famous Electric Horses. Every ride was different and exciting. People of all ages could enjoy the variety of fun and forget the fact that America was going through a major depression. Many of the people had no jobs.

Coney Island had swim clubs that you could join for the whole summer. Washington Baths, Brighton Beach Baths, Manhattan Beach, and Raven Hall. They had pools which members could use and an exit through which you could go on the beach if you wanted to swim in the ocean. The key to your locker would get you on the beach and back. On a hot summer day up to one million people would go to the beach in Coney Island to try and keep cool. It was hot on the sand, but you could always go into the cool water and get refreshed. I rarely went to the beach because my skin is so white that I get burned in ten minutes. However, all the young people would meet at Bay 2 in the Brighton Beach area. I remember when Pepsi Cola was introduced. Airplanes with trailing signs advertised the introduction. It was about 1936.

Every Tuesday night at 9 o'clock there was a marvelous fireworks display. It drew thousands of people to the boardwalk and the crowds could enjoy the bowery where there was a variety if amusements and games. Mrs. Stahl's Knishes on Coney Island Avenue was a favorite, and of course, there was Nathan's Famous Hot dogs. Nathan Handwerker started in Feltman's in the early 1900s.

He was a waiter or had some other job, but he realized the potential of the frankfurter, and opened his own place at Surf Avenue and Stillwell Avenue, just across the street from all the subway lines. Nathan's sold a 12 inch, all- beef frankfurter for only a nickel. With mustard and sauerkraut it was a meal. Nathan's also had hamburgers, French Fries, Chow Mein, and fruit drinks. They were all only a nickel. Across the way, alongside the hot dog stand was a custard stand with three flavors-vanilla, chocolate, and strawberry. Boy, were they good! Nathan's also sold sweet corns. It was truly a glutton's paradise. Whitey Reisman, my brother Bernie's friend loved the frankfurters so much that he used all of his 35 cents on franks and had to walk home. After all the years that have passed, Nathan's Famous is still dishing out the frankfurters and French fries. They may be smaller, and cost a little more, but they are still a big draw, and one of the outstanding names associated with Coney Island. Every year they have a hot dog eating contest on July 4th at Nathan's. The original Feltman's had entertainers who became famous in radio, television, and the movies. I refer to Eddie Cantor and Jimmy Durante.

Coney Island was also known for its sporting events. Boxing, bicycle racing, wrestling in Stauch's Arena (which I attended several times). Gino Garibaldi and Ernie Dusek are two of the names I remember. The roller coaster rides were famous. The Cyclone and the Mile-Sky-Chaser were thrilling rides that everyone enjoyed. So was the Parachute Jump. The Carousel on West 5th Street near the New York Aquarium was popular and a Battem Cage was on the fringe of Surf Avenue. I remember in the years after I was married, taking my family to Coney Island for some of Nathan's goodies. I saw a crowd gathered at the Battem Cage where you could hit baseballs that were pitched from a machine. I noticed a pink Cadillac convertible parked in front. It was Sugar Ray Robinson, the great champion boxer. He was trying his luck at the cage.

It was a simpler time. No photographers were nagging at the champ. He was a great guy and talked to all of us without an air of importance. He was just a plain guy who made good. Pound for pound, he may have been the greatest boxer of all time. Rocky Graziano lived right behind my house after World War II. His home was on Ocean Parkway and ours was on East 7th Street. He used to walk his dogs (Boxers) around the block, and I would see him occasionally.

In the winter my brother Eugene used to go fishing for Whiting on Steeplechase Pier. It was very cold. He put on two pairs of pants, a couple of sweaters, and a heavy mackinaw. To keep his hands warm he wore heavy gloves. He wasn't the only one who liked to fish for Whiting. The pier was full, and you had to stake out your spot early or you would be shut out. One day I decided to surprise him and go to the pier. I started out by taking the trolley in the gully on Bath Avenue. I was waiting for the trolley for half an hour. When it finally came, the conductor zoomed right by me. I was so small he didn't see me. I finally got a trolley to stop (not before I cried in desperation). When I got to Coney Island I went to Nathan's and bought a bag of franks and French Fries. When I arrived at the pier and found my brother Gene he was happy to warm up with the hot dogs and the fries. He usually caught a sack of Whiting. Our cat, Tiger, was the beneficiary of Eugene's love for fishing. He would eat four or five fish before he gave up and went back to his favorite sleeping place.

The Balloon Tire Bike

The most disappointing thing of my young life was that my parents never bought me a bicycle. I mean a two-wheeler. I did have a tricycle, which I raced down the street at top speed. In fact, I tilted it into the position where I was actually riding on only two wheels. I must have been about 13 or 14 years old when the Stillwell Theatre sponsored a contest to see who could be the Hi-Li champion. The Hi-Li was simply a wooden paddle which had a small rubber ball stapled to it. You hit the ball and the thin rubber string would allow it to stretch out and return to the paddle. It was a big thing with the kids in the neighborhood. I became an expert in Hi-Li tricks and could paddle the ball for as long as a half hour without missing.

I entered the preliminary contest, which was held outside the theatre. Most of the entrants were not very good, and I easily won the first round, which had a prize of a box of Oh Henry candy bars. The semi-finals were held just before my family was leaving the city for the summer. We went up to Kerhonkson in the Catskill Mountains for eight weeks every year. I had no problem winning the next round, which eliminated another group of hopefuls. This time the first prize was a pair of Union Hardware roller skates, but I had my eye on the grand prize of the final competition, which was a balloon tire Schwinn bicycle. That pitted me up against the best Hi-Li players in Brooklyn. There were only five contestants in the finals. The date was July 30th, and I was up in the country for the whole month practicing and refining my style of play. Some players hit the ball straight up in the air, but I found it easier to use a side arm method.

I went back to the city and bought a brand new, deluxe Hi-Li paddle. I went back all by myself. I took the old New York, Ontario & Western Railroad into New York and prepared myself for the big day. If I won and became champion, I would fulfill my dream of owning a bicycle. The grand prize was a beautiful, balloon tire Schwinn bicycle. It was a very hot day, and there were several hundred people who came out to watch the contest.

    I started out very calmly and entered a groove where the ball was behaving beautifully. My opponents looked nervous and after about fifteen minutes two of them dropped out. Ten minutes later another one dropped out. That left only two of us. I was still steady and hitting the ball gently, but my opponent was erratic, nervous, and hitting the ball up at a 45 degree angle. I was confident that I could win If I just kept doing my thing. Forty minutes passed and we were still going. Sweat was pouring down into my eyes, but I didn't let it keep me from my goal. At the 45th minute, my ball and its thin rubber string that was attached to it didn't return to the paddle. It broke and landed in the gutter. I had failed to realize my dream of owning a bicycle. However, I was consoled by the fact that it was not my fault. It was strictly the result of a breakdown of the equipment I was using. It was disappointing for a young boy to be denied his dream, but it was just another lesson one has to learn while growing up. You have to learn how to be a good loser.

The Accordion Fascination

From the time I was ten years old, I played the ukulele. I learned how to play by watching Georgie Katzman, on Pataukunk Road, in Kerhonkson, New York. My family spent our summers at Dunn's farm. One room with kitchen privileges-$35 dollars for the whole summer.

Georgiie Katzman had a guitar with only the last four strings. These are tuned just like a uke. It was really a tenor guitar. It didn't take long for me to learn a few chords and play the popular songs of the day like "Bei Mir Bist du Schoen," "Dinah," "Lazy Bones," and "Side by Side." I now own a Martin concert ukulele and play it for my own pleasure.

When I was thirteen years old I graduated from Junior High school. I volunteered to entertain at a talent show in the school auditorium before hundreds of my fellow graduates. It was my first attempt at singing before a large audience. I played "Sam, You Made the Pants too Long," and "Robins and Roses." I enjoyed my effort and received a loud ovation. But more important than that was my fascination with a young girl who played "Lady of Spain" on the accordion. I must have that, I thought.

When I went home, I told my mother that I would like to take accordion lessons. She consented, and for two dollars a lesson we engaged a teacher, Mr. Schiff, who came to my house once a week. I started with a 12 bass accordion, which I outgrew almost immediately. It only had major chords. Within a few weeks I was ready for my Anelli, a 120 bass accordion which was billed as the lightest accordion in the world. It was imported from Italy. The fascination with the accordion lasted about three years. I played all the music at my oldest brother's wedding, and enjoyed playing at family gatherings, and a few paid gigs such as anniversary parties, etc. The one appearance that I remember clearly was the dedication of a large billboard of servicemen's names on the wall of the Stillwell Theatre at 86th Street and 24th Avenue in Brooklyn. The neighborhood turned out in force to see the names of their loved ones listed on the sign. My two brothers Bernard and Eugene were on the list.

I played my accordion at this ceremony, and everyone sang as I played, "God Bless America." I was only sixteen years old. It was the last time I played the accordion at any large gathering. My love affair with the accordion was over, but I still get a thrill when I hear a tango played on the accordion such as "El Choclo," "Two Guitars," and other classics like "Monti's Czardas," or "The Jolly Caballero."

Lafayette High School

My years at Lafayette High School were great. I was very young, fourteen and fifteen years of age. One day I saw a notice on the bulletin board in the gymnasium announcing tryouts for the first athletic team at the school, the soccer team. We were fortunate to have the best coach in the city. He was Simon Yudell. Sy Yudell always had winning soccer teams at New Utrecht High School from the late 1920s through the 1930s. New Utrecht was always playing James Monroe High School of the Bronx for the P.S.A.L. championship. I knew nothing about soccer, and most of the students trying out for the team were also new to the sport. It was the fall of 1939, and most of the experienced players came from Italy, Latin America, South America, or other foreign countries.

We had no soccer field so our home field was Ulmer Park. Old timers will remember that firemen and policemen in the 1920s and 1930s would have their picnics at Ulmer Park. It was an oversized field with an uneven turf and many sand pits. These holes turned into mud pits or outright lakes if we had a big rainstorm. However, that is all we had and it was exciting to be able to play on the school team. We all had to walk about half a mile traversing the Belt Parkway which was just being built. The concrete and steel base of the road's structure was being laid at this time.

The day of the tryouts was sunny, and a giant turnout of about 150 young men were there. Coach Yudell with a mini-megaphone and a whistle assembled the group on one side of the field. He announced that it was going to be difficult to select 20 men out of the group assembled. He asked,

"How many of you have ever played soccer? "
Only about five men raised their hands.

"All right," he said

"When I blow the whistle, I want you all to start running to the other side of the field and back. Don't stop until I blow the whistle again."

The field at Ulmer Park was about 100 yards long. Many football and soccer games were played there by high schools, semi-pro, and club teams. It was a long field.

Sy Yudell blew the whistle and the large group of hopefuls started to run back and forth down the field. After ten or fifteen minutes, men began to fall down and otherwise drop out of the competition. It was plain to see that Yudell's idea was to find a group of 25 men who had the stamina to run back and forth without collapsing. He didn't have time to train a group of men and get them into playing condition. Soccer is a grueling sport which entails non-stop running for an hour and a half. It didn't take too long before the Lafayette soccer team began to take shape. The last 25 men who were on their feet were on the team. The rest of the guys went home.

Now the coach began the job of teaching the fundamentals of soccer. We learned passing, trapping, heading, kicking, and Sy Yudell's favorite word, "cohesion." It was simply teamwork that won ball games, and Yudell knew how to inspire a team with the winning spirit. We had great teams at Lafayette, and I had the distinction of being a member of the first Lafayette High School soccer team. It made me proud. I went on to play at Brooklyn College, and in the Army (more about that later).

I also tried out for the baseball team, which didn't happen until I was in the 7th term of high school. Baseball was my first love. Almost every kid in Brooklyn with athletic ability dreamed of playing for the Brooklyn Dodgers. Coach Lefkowitz had tryouts for the team, and I was a senior when the varsity was chosen.

"Red," said Lefkowitz, "you are one of the best hitters and fielders out here, but I am trying to build a team for the future. You are a senior, and I need freshmen. You'll be playing for Tubby Raskin at Brooklyn College next year." It was a great disappointment, but I knew the coach was right. He fielded good teams at Lafayette, which produced Sandy Koufax, Fred Wilpon (owner of the New York Mets), John Franco, and many others who went on to fame in the major leagues.

For the most part the guys in my neighborhood were in good shape. The whole block was represented on Lafayette High School's soccer teams. Soccer is great because you have to run for an hour and a half. This leads to an aerobic level of exercise that builds a strong heart. The heart is a muscle that beats 100,000 times a day. The valves open and close 38 million times a year. The foundation that soccer builds in your early years can truly lead to a vascular system which stays with you for most of your life. I played in high school, college, and the Army during the war. I am sure that the benefits will last all my life. The fact that I had ten frostbitten toes were no impediment to my playing soccer when I returned to college after the war. The only after- effect was a lack of circulation in the toes. The tissues were destroyed beyond repair.

The Day That Will Live in Infamy

Seventy-two years ago, December 7th, 1941, marks the date of the civilized world's most dastardly military attack in history. The Empire of Japan, in a display of hubris, attacked major areas of the Pacific Ocean with a well-orchestrated plan to dominate that part of the world. The attack was planned weeks before its implementation.

The transparent deception of the Japanese government was plain to see. One hour after the attack on Pearl Harbor, on the island of Oahu, Hawaii, the Japanese ambassador was in Washington. He delivered a formal reply to President Roosevelt stating that" it would be useless to continue negotiation."

On December 7th Japan attacked Malaya.
On December 7th Japan attacked Hong Kong.
On December 7th Japan attacked Guam.
On December 7th Japan attacked the Phillipine Islands.
On December 7th Japan attacked Wake Island.
On December 7th Japan attacked Midway Island.

"Useless to continue negotiations, indeed!" It was a sneak attack, planned and developed over a long period of time. It was so bad that we lost most of our battleships. The major ships that were destroyed and sunk in port were: the Arizona, the Virginia, the West Virginia, and the Oklahoma. The irony of this event cannot but warn future generations of the perfidy and arrogance of some nations of the world. The very aircraft carriers and the battleships of the Japanese Navy were built using the steel scrap that we sold them when the Third Avenue L was dismantled.   The Japanese sent 360 fighter-bombers and 10 aircraft carriers against a peaceful nation that was sleeping, disarmed, and woefully unprepared to defend itself. We had just experienced a major depression. After the stock market crashed in 1929 there were millions of unemployed and President Roosevelt's preoccupation was his attempt to revive the nation's economy. He sponsored many government programs such as the CCC (Civilian Conservation Corps),the WPA (Works Progress Administration), the NRA (National Recovery Act), and many others. This was not lost on the enemy who sought to strike us when we were not at our strongest. However, it proved to be just what our country needed to jolt us out of the depression. Gearing up for war with an enemy that had attacked us united the nation as never before.

On that day, December 7th, 1941, 3,400 Americans were killed and many thousands were wounded. President Roosevelt reminded us in his stirring speech on December 8th, 1941 before a joint session of congress.

"Remember," he said, "the character of the onslaught against us." He said further,

"That no matter how long it takes, the American people in their righteous might will win through to the inevitable victory."

He concluded,

"With confidence in the future, and the unbounding determination of our people, we will gain the inevitable triumph, so help us God!"

And finally he said,

"A state of war has existed between the Japanese Empire and the United States."

Admiral Yamamoto expressed the fear that, "We have awakened a slumbering giant." Was he ever right! When America is united in spirit and purpose, almost nothing is impossible for us to achieve. This is an object lesson that should not be forgotten today. When President Roosevelt called the attack by Japan "a day that will live in infamy" it rallied the nation. We were united. There were no democrats or republicans. We were Americans. We were attacked, and we pledged to win the war. Our terms were simple and direct—nothing less than unconditional surrender. When we declared war on Japan, Germany declared war on the United States. Italy was also part of the axis that lined up against the United States. The three dictators, Hitler, Mussolini, and Japan's Tojo were joined in their attempt to defeat the United States and the United Kingdom. After the invasion of the Soviet Union by Germany, the Russians joined the Allies.

The day after President Roosevelt's speech, December 8th 1941, I ran to the post office to register for the draft. There were tears of anger in my eyes as I ran as fast as I could to add my name to the growing list of men who wanted to fight for their great country.

I graduated from Lafayette High School on January, 1941. I had just turned sixteen. My first two years of high school were at New Utrecht. It was crowded. I never did get to the main building, but spent my time in annexes P.S. 180 and P.S. 105. We were all Brooklyn dodger fans. The principal of P.S. 105 closed down the school on opening day so we could all go to Ebbets Field.

When Lafayette High School was ready for occupancy, the fifth term students who lived in the neighborhood were transferred from New Utrecht to Lafayette. It was a brand new school. The paint was still wet when we started classes. I felt great because I lived so close to the school that I could go home for lunch. I had a pass which permitted me to leave the school and return to my afternoon classes.

Brooklyn College

It didn't take long for me to realize that college was different from high school. My problem adjusting to this new life was that I was only sixteen years old. I wasn't really ready for this change. All my friends were two years behind me, and were still in high school. I was like a fish out of water.

Brooklyn College in 1941 was a spanking new school. The buildings on Bedford avenue were opened in 1937, and all the students who were going to the school downtown at Willoughby Street were moved into the new facility. Brooklyn College opened on October 18, 1937, accommodated 1,500 students, and was erected at a cost of $5,500,000. The admission was free, but the requirement was a high school grade average of about 90. It was worth noting that when I attended Brooklyn College, it was rated 6th in the country academically, higher than Harvard University.

I immediately tried out for the junior varsity baseball team. Tom Harrington was the coach. I made the team without a problem, but I didn't distinguish myself as a player. It was the following year, when I tried out for the varsity that I remember clearly. Tubby Raskin was the coach, and he had a large group of men line up and take a few swings at the ball. I was nervous as I stepped up to the plate. I took three swings at the ball and missed each one. However, Tubby liked the way I stood at the plate and obviously saw the way I swung the bat that showed I could hit the ball. As it turned out, I never really got the chance to show my ability on the field. The only opportunity I had to do anything was in April, 1943, right before I went into the Army. Tubby sent a team of junior varsity players up to Lewisohn Stadium to play City College. I was the captain of the group and we won 3 to 1. I got three hits and did well in center field. But it was the end of the road for me. My dream of playing professional baseball clashed with my duty to my country. It just wasn't meant to be.

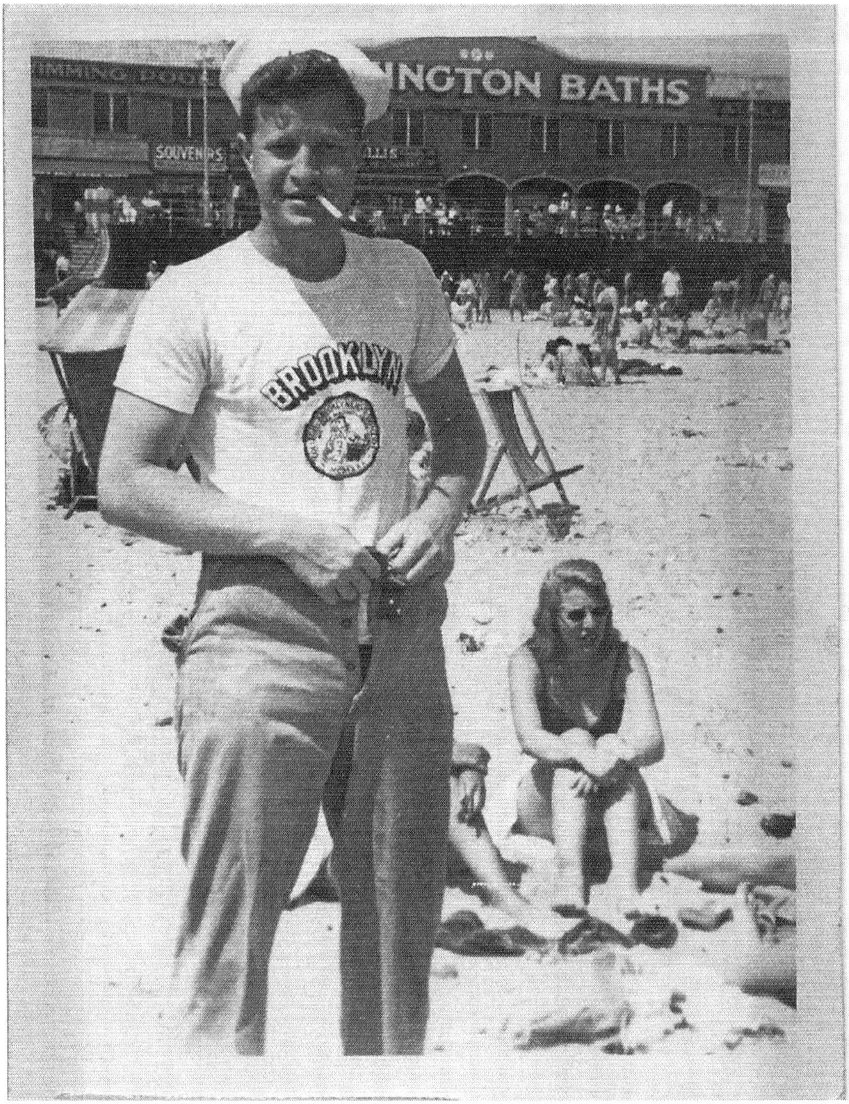
NGTON BATHS
SOUVENIRS
BROOKLYN

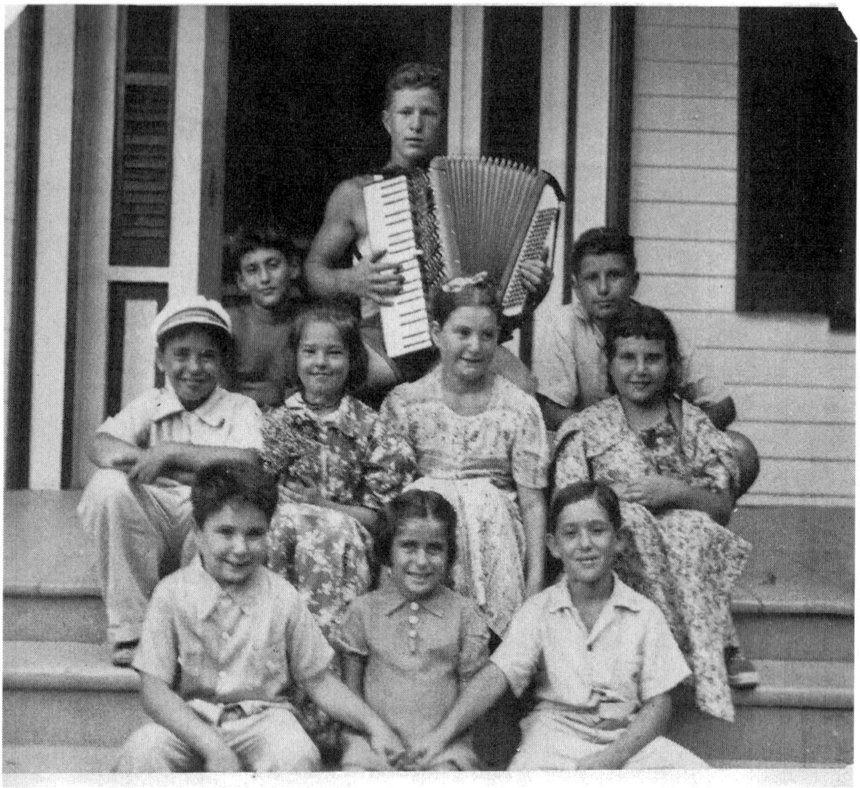

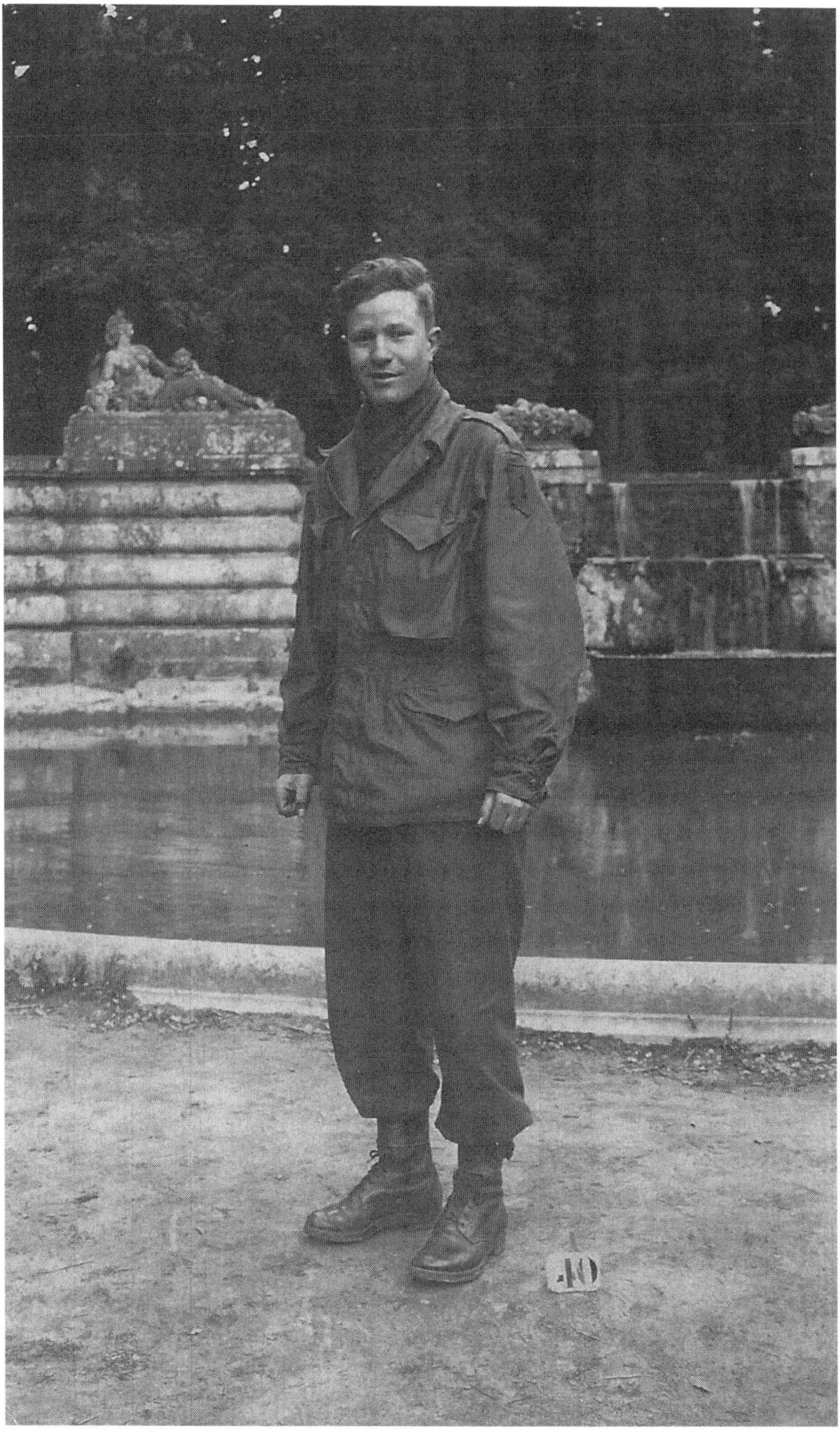
40

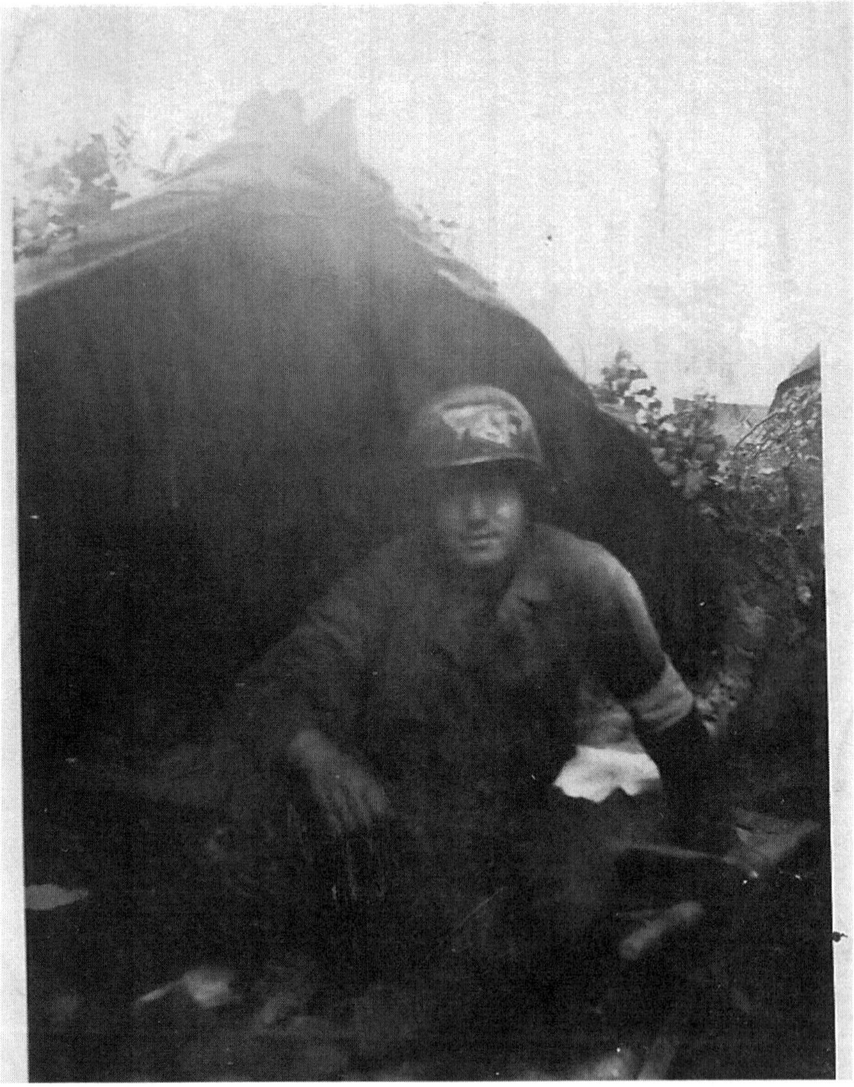

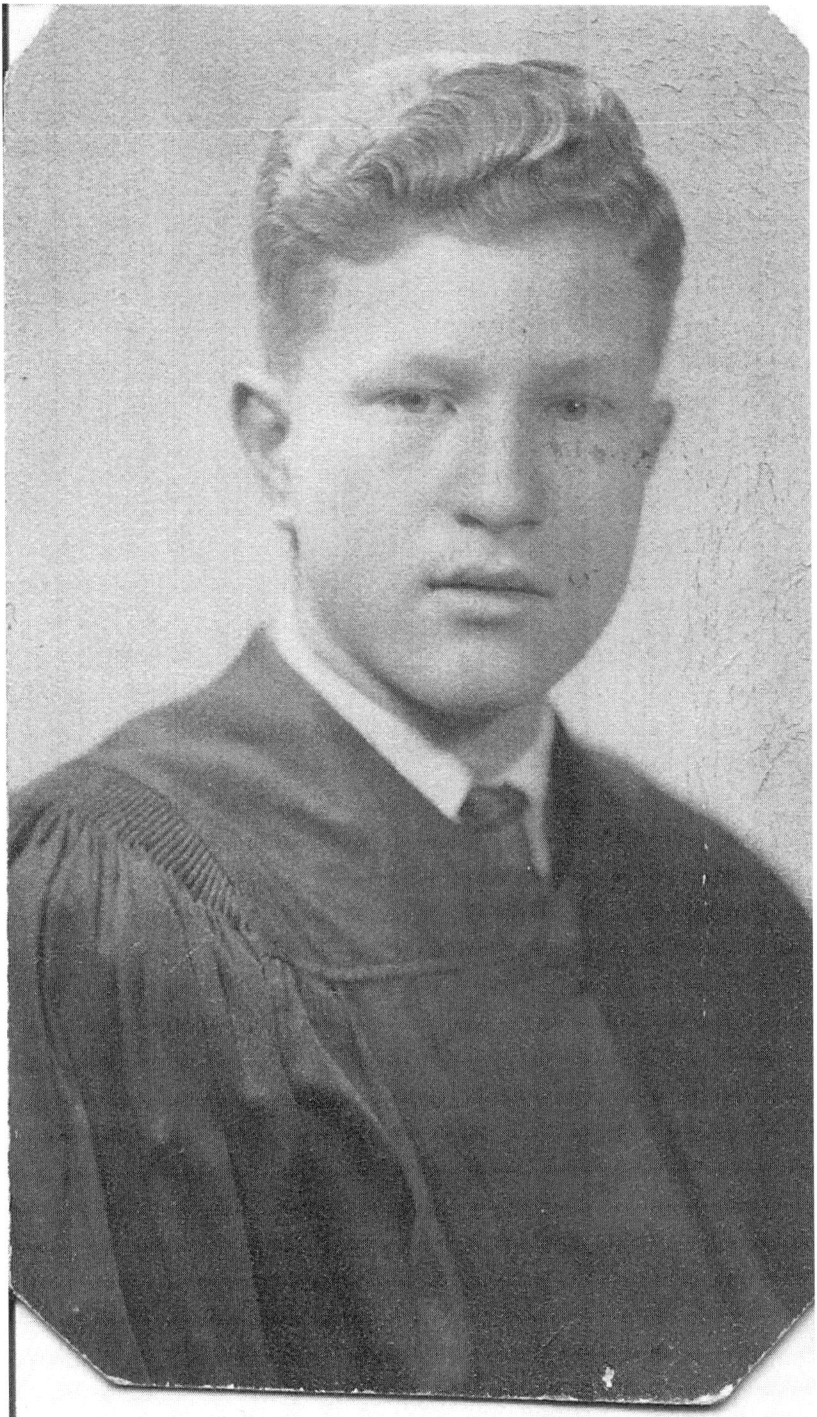

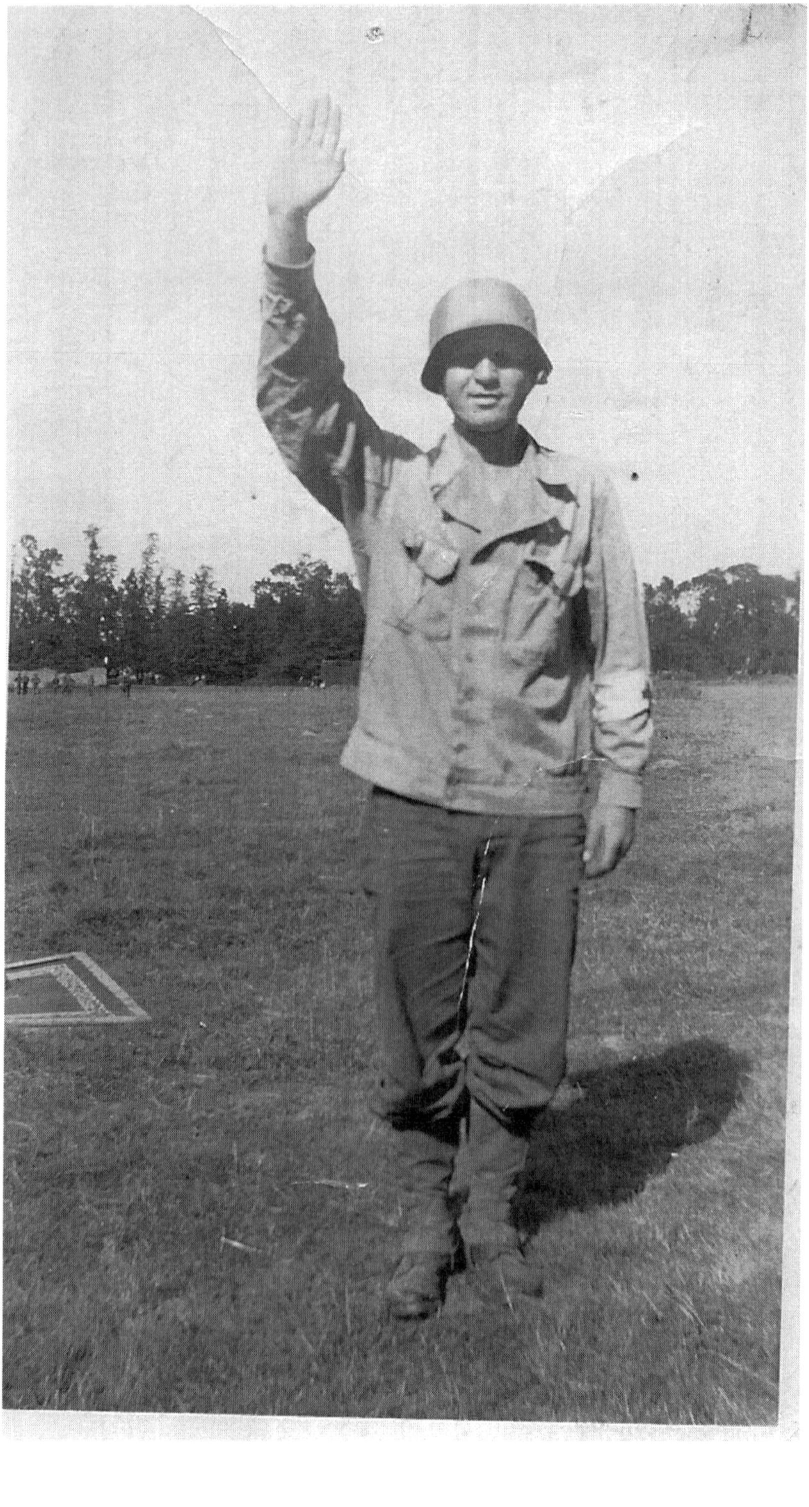

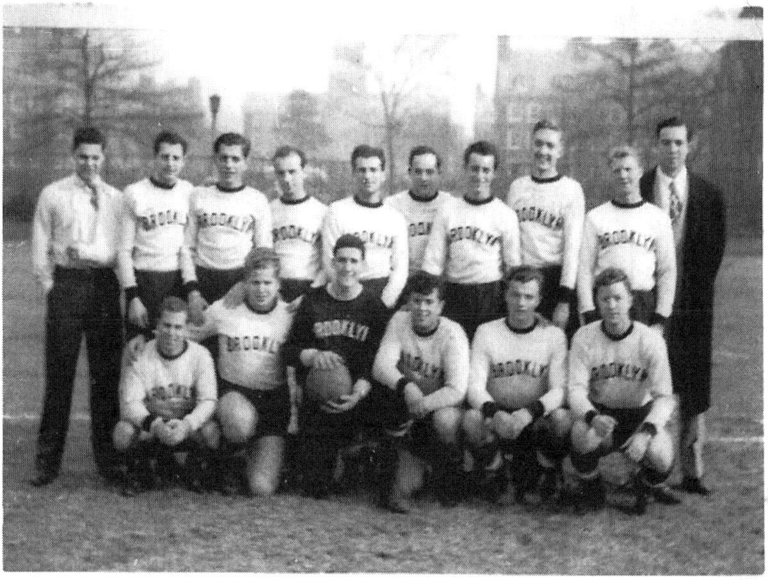

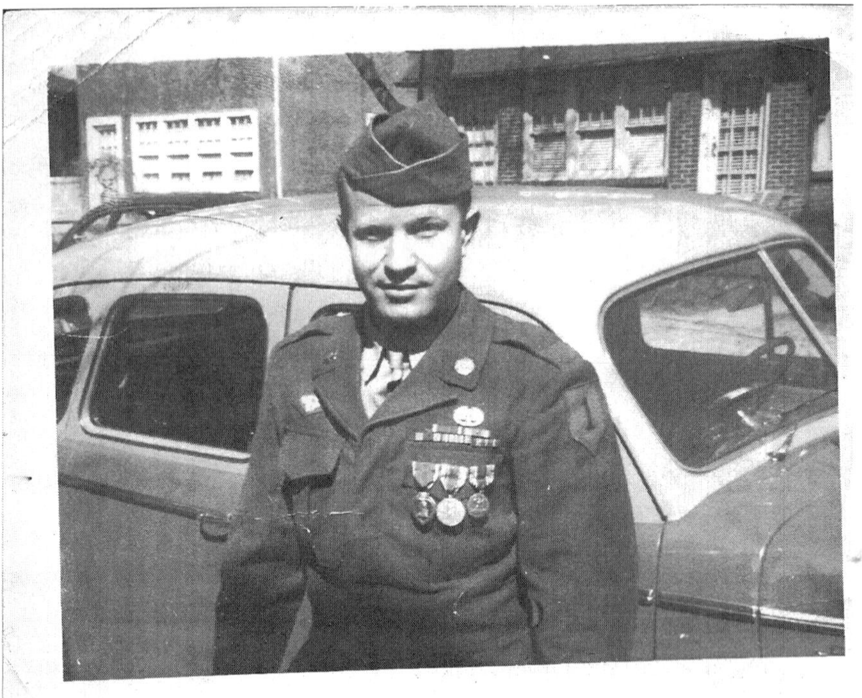

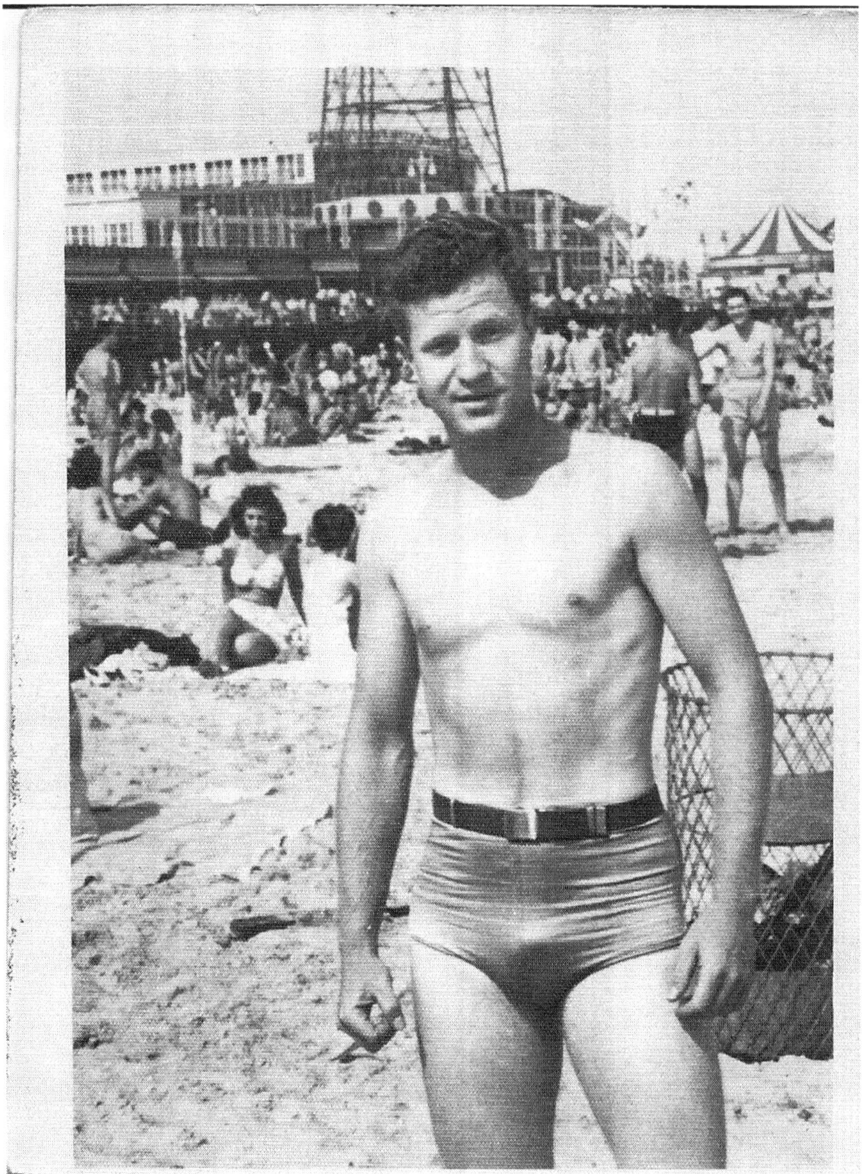

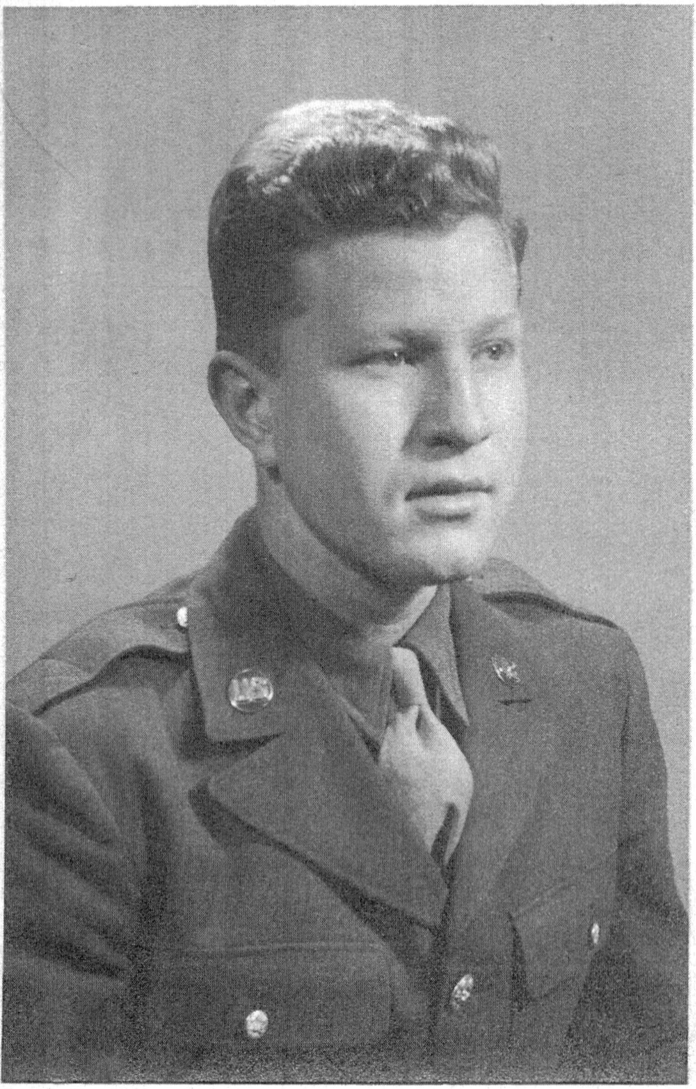

Fort Dix

When my mother saw the bus leave from the Benson theatre in Brooklyn, she didn't cry or display any weakness. It was characteristic of her inner strength, her spirit, and her eternal optimism. Her youngest son was leaving, and it never dawned on me that I may never see her again. I might not come home again. Can anyone understand the anguish that a mother feels when her son goes off to war?

My two older brothers were already in the service. Gene was in the air force in South Dakota and Bernie was at Fort Benjamin Harrison in Indiana in the finance school. Now a third star would have to be put in the window of our home. It was a common sight during the war for a home to display a small satin banner in the window, with one star for each person in the service. Both of my brothers ended up in Italy. I didn't see them until the war was over.

I was headed for Fort Dix in New Jersey. It was a major distribution center in the northeast. Thousands of G.I.s were processed, sorted into specialties (based on educational background or their job experience) and shipped out to various camps all over the country. It was a vast undertaking to help young civilians learn how the Army works. You have to grow up fast. It was wartime, and the whole country was adjusting to a new way of life.

One incident stands out in my mind. A large parade ground with hundreds of new recruits were doing calisthenics. The officer leading the exercises stopped the jumping jacks and the push-ups and asked the question.

"Who knows how to take short hand?
Twelve men raised their hands. Ostensibly, they thought it would lead to a good job in an office.

"O.K.! you guys follow the sergeant. We're short-handed in the kitchen!"

When I left the cradle of my mother's arms, and entered the United States Army, it was the beginning of a new life. A stage that William Shakespeare included in his "All the world's a stage, and all the men and women merely players. First the infant, mewling and puking in his nurse's arms. Then, the whining schoolboy, creeping like snail, unwillingly to school. Then, the lover, sighing like furnace, etc." Then the soldier! I made it. I am now a soldier. The army will now educate me. My superiors will teach me the rules, the etiquette, and the nomenclature that the army demands of its soldiers.

The first thing I learned at Fort Dix was that when you see an officer you must salute. The proper way to salute is to line up your fingers and your thumb. Then you place your hand at a 45 degree angle over your eyebrow and snap it quickly out in front of you. I learned this lesson three days after I arrived at Fort Dix. I was told to deliver two buckets of lime to a certain person. When I did so, I put my arm around this warrant officer's shoulder. His bars were similar to a lieutenant's. This officer stiffened up immediately and said,

"Soldier, he said, do you see these bars?" pointing to his shoulder.

"Yes," I said meekly.

"Well, when you see those bars, even if you are 100 yards away, I expect to see you salute! Do you get that?"

"Yes sir," I said.
Boy, that was a lesson I'll never forget.
It reminds me of a joke that a U.S.O> comedian used to tell. It seems that two soldiers were walking down the street and a truck rolled by. One of the soldiers saluted the driver.

"What are you doing? Why are you saluting? said one of the men.

"The sign said general hauling!" answered the other.

Fort Dix was one of the busiest reception centers of World War II. It processed hundreds of thousands of soldiers from the northeastern states. Camp Upton on Long Island was another reception center that put civilians through the grinder and turned out soldiers. Men were put through basic training and taught the rules, but the major job of Fort Dix was to relocate the men to bases where the grueling basic training was performed. It could be infantry, paratroopers, tank corps, air force, etc. Men were assigned to their future posts based on their education, occupations, and their preference and selection. A joke that made the rounds was that if a man greased trucks in civilian life, he was a perfect candidate to be a cook!

I remember very little about my short stay at Fort Dix, but I recall a lieutenant asking if anyone knew anything about first aid. I had just finished a course in health and physiology at Brooklyn College, so I volunteered to lecture several classes of soldiers on first aid. Little did I realize that I would be putting my knowledge to work running a dispensary in Belgium, and then patching up the wounded on the battlefield in the Ardennes forest.

At Fort Dix the new recruits were taught many things that the Army requires. Nothing stands out in my memory more than discipline. Close order drill is an exercise that demands attention to orders. You have to know your right leg from your left leg. When you hear the order, "forward march!" you start off with your left foot. If you don't, you'll be out of step with the rest of the troops. Some of the orders you learn are: forward march, detail halt, to the left flank march, to the right flank march, to the rear march, double time march, right oblique march, left oblique march, column left march, column right march, at ease, and attention!

This exercise demands attention and precision, and the officer barking orders is trying to trip you up. An infantryman has to learn how to take care of his rifle. I remember the old Army man who was lecturing us on the M1 rifle.

"This is the butt," he said, pointing to the stock of the rifle.

"This is the barrel!." You must keep it oiled up and clean all the time.

"The site is where you look when you are aiming at a target."

You are treated like a kindergarten child. But you must learn these vital things. "The nomenclature" defines the parts of a rifle. When you are issued an M1 rifle, you have to keep it clean, so that on inspection you don't pick up extra duty.

I was assigned to the headquarters company of the 23rd Replacement Depot. We eventually would be charged with the responsibility of training replacements that were needed on the front lines. We therefore took the same training as any infantryman. We took long marches with full field packs. We studied map reading and went to the firing range and practiced grenade throwing. We learned hand-to-hand combat and had bayonet drill. The scary exercise was crawling through the obstacle course. We had to avoid getting tangled up in the barbed wire, while live ammunition was sailing overhead. These and many other disciplines were part of basic training. After several weeks at Fort Dix, the headquarters company of the 23rd Replacement Depot, part of the First army, was deployed to Camp Sutton, North Carolina, which was located near Charlotte.

Carolina in the Morning

"Nothing could be finer than to be in Carolina in the Morning." But not at 3.30 A.M. in the morning, when my first sergeant blows a whistle right in my ear, and lifts my bed up and slams it down hard on the floor. This is to make sure you are awake and ready to report for K.P. (kitchen police) at officers' mess. The cook then sits you down with a case of eggs and orders you to break them into a giant kettle to get ready for scrambling. When you are finished with that job, you have to peel a couple of fifty pound bags of potatoes. This detail is just one of the many jobs that were part of the growing up process in the army.

My company was moved from Fort Dix to Camp Sutton, near Charlotte, North Carolina. It was only a few weeks before we were moved again. This time it was a more permanent base for the remainder of my basic training. We moved to Camp Butner. It wasn't too long before I realized that K.P., ration breakdown, guard duty in the PX (Post Exchange), wasn't for me. Our commanding officer, Colonel Moore, was a sports lover and I joined the soccer team, and the battalion boxing team. This was the best way to avoid getting assigned to extra duty. There was soccer practice and boxing exhibitions that took up most of my spare time. In addition to these sports, the camp had an excellent football team which toured North Carolina and played other Army, Marine, and Air Force bases in Greensboro, Asheville, Cherry Point, and others. Charlie Trippi, a pro football star was stationed at the Greensboro Air Force Base. The games were terrific, and many of the boys at Butner got to travel the state in buses to root for our team.

One outstanding experience that I recall was when our soccer team played the Navy at Chapel Hill, North Carolina. My team was composed of mostly ethnic Americans who had played in their native countries when they were young. I was unique, in that American-born soccer players were rare in 1943. We had no uniforms, no soccer shoes, and no shin guards. Every player had a different shirt, regular Army shoes, and we were forced to practice on an uneven dirt lot that was the only available place. We walked out onto the field, a motley crew, with no hope of success. But we loved the game.

The navy team filed out onto the well-manicured pitch, with well-defined sidelines, penalty area, and goal posts that had a net behind them to catch the ball. The team had lovely, new, black and gold uniforms, new soccer shoes, shin guards, etc. It looked like a mismatch. The game started and it immediately became apparent that you didn't need a fancy uniform to be a good soccer player. I had experience in high school and with the superior play of our team we beat the Navy 3 to 1. I remember the Navy coach saying to me,

"Where did you learn to play so well?"

"I played for Sy Yudell in New York for two years."

"No wonder, said the Navy coach. "Sy Yudell is one of the best soccer coaches in the country."

His reputation had spread around the small fraternity of soccer coaches who had an association that would meet annually to survey the progress that soccer was making in the United States. In the years that followed, the famous Brazilian star, Pele, brought his magic to a professional soccer league that developed into a major sport. Now soccer is very popular in all public, high schools, and colleges throughout the country.

My boxing improved very quickly with each match and with continuous sparring. It increased my confidence and created a reputation among my fellow soldiers who knew that I could hold my own in a fight. This was important for obvious reasons. No one wanted to mess with me.

I am of the Jewish faith, and was brought up in a kosher home. For many years I conducted Sabbath services in the synagogue where I had my Bar Mitzvah. I continued to run the services until I entered the army. The Jewish chaplain came to Camp Butner once a month, and he asked me to conduct the Friday night services for the three weeks that he was away at other camps. I agreed. Every Friday night was G.I. night when the barracks were scrubbed down and the windows were washed. I arranged with my sergeant to scrub down the floor around my bed and clean the windows near my area.

One Friday night, as I was preparing to leave for the chapel to conduct the service, I overheard a soldier named, Bailey, a big, rawboned, six foot five inch tall guy from Kentucky say something anti-Semitic. He probably was subject to the fairy tale that Jews had horns. I doubt that he had ever seen a Jew before he left his home environment. Well, he was saying in a voice that was loud enough for me to hear,

"There goes that Jew bastard again leaving us to clean the barracks without him!"

I wheeled around immediately and instinctively grabbed his shirt by the collar and lifted this big hillbilly off the floor, and said,

"If you have anything you'd like to say to me, let's go out behind the barracks and settle it like a man!"

The blood drained out of his face and he was as white as a ghost. He sheepishly replied,

"I didn't mean anything, I don't want to settle anything. Let's not fight. I understand that you do your share of the cleaning. I'm O.K. with that. Is it all right with you?"

With that, I turned around to face the 25 men in the barracks who had witnessed the whole thing, and said,

"And that goes for any one of you that has a problem with me, and the fact that I'm helping other men in this camp pray to their God! I'll meet you all out behind the barracks one at a time!"

Well, I wasn't prepared for the response to my emotional tirade. It might have been the best thing that could have happened to me. Each soldier in the barracks came over to me and shook my hand and congratulated me for the stand I took. From that day forward, I didn't have a problem with anyone in the company.

Basic Training

It didn't matter where you were training, it was all the same.. We were years behind the enemy in every way. We had to whip our soldiers into peak condition as fast as we could. Our factories began to churn out equipment; planes, ships, guns, ammunition, etc. It was an urgent need to preserve our way of life. The people responded. As a soldier, I had to do my part.

Several months of intensive activity followed, including rifle practice at the firing range. I worked the pits and learned the language-bullseye, Maggie's drawers, etc. Long marches that strengthened the muscles all over our body and built endurance were part of the physical aspect of our training. Lectures of all kinds tended to the mental and psychological part of our program. All the while, the Army saw to it that you learned the disciplines and attention to detail whether it was making a bed, straightening out your foot locker, or taking your rifle apart and reassembling it. Some men could do it blindfolded in a few minutes. You never knew when you might have to do it in the dark. The barrel of the rifle had to be oiled and kept clean. Inspections kept us on our toes. If we wanted a week-end pass, we couldn't afford to foul up.

The obstacle course was a scary operation because you had to crawl under barbed wire while live ammunition was sailing overhead. Bayonet drill was a serious and necessary course to prepare for the possibility of hand-to-hand combat. Hand grenade practice was important because it involved a technique that is different from throwing a baseball. After pulling the pin, you have to wait several seconds before you throw the grenade at your target. It is not Hollywood! It's the real thing. And it was the real thing we were preparing for.

I was able to secure a three-day pass for the Jewish New Year. My friend Jerry Shapiro was at Camp Croft in Spartanburg, South Carolina, which was a bus ride from my base. I thought it would be a great idea to surprise him with a visit. An incident happened on one of the local buses in South Carolina that stands out in my memory. This was long before Rosa Parks and her defiance of the Jim Crow laws made her famous. I boarded a bus that was crowded, and a black woman who was seated at the front saw me standing near her. She immediately arose from her seat and made an attempt to walk to the back of the bus. I was not accustomed to have older women giving me their seat in either a bus or train. I insisted that she remain in her seat, to the discomfort of the white people who were sitting nearby.

When I finally located the barracks where my friend was billeted, I walked in and there he was, mopping the floor. We had a warm reunion and spent a couple of days together before I had to return to my base. It was a good break from our rigorous routine. We were so tired that when we were told to take a ten minute break, we could actually sleep for ten minutes, even if we were on a pile of rocks. I said good bye to my best friend and left. He was in the 36th Division that landed at Anzio, Italy. I didn't see Jerry again until the war was over.

As the year 1943 wore on, it was getting close to the time when all our training was about to pay off. We were ready. The rumors about where we were going were answered when we learned that the company was leaving in late December for Camp Myles Standish near Boston. I was given a 24-hour pass on December 30th. It was just enough time to go home to Brooklyn, New York. I spent a few precious hours with my family and then said good bye to them.

My uncle Sam Gellman, who was a World War I veteran, and knew that it was possible I may never return. volunteered to accompany me to Penn Station. He spent the last few hours with me before the train pulled out. I can still see the sad look on his face. He was concerned about my safety. I shall never forget his gesture. It was cold in Boston. It was so cold that the ink froze up on the pot-bellied stove we had in the barracks. We didn't do too much while we were waiting for our ship to arrive. We did have a gas-mask exercise, and I had time to go to the library. I took out two books, "Mein Kampf" by Adolph Hitler, and "The Magic Mountain" by Thomas Mann. Our ship pulled out of Boston harbor on January 1, 1944.

Over There

It was obvious that we were sailing for Europe. The ship we had was a Liberty ship that Henry Kaiser was building by the hundreds. The German submarines were sinking freighters and troopships, so we had to snake our way across the North Atlantic to avoid the U boats. The ocean was rough and the ship was small. Many of us got seasick. It took 10 days if pitching and yawing before we reached Liverpool, England. Between bouts of seasickness, I was able to read both books I took out of Camp Myles Standish's library. The 23rd Replacement Depot set up shop at Houndstone and Lufton barracks outside of the town of Yeovil, in Somerset, Southern England. It was January, and it was cold and wet.

Almost imperceptibly, the months passed by as thousands of soldiers were kept in shape with long marches and other physical exercises. However, there was some time which was spent indulging in sports. I was on the battalion softball team, and was fortunate enough to win a few games with a timely hit here and there. But these moments were just a diversion. All of England was a staging area. It was a platform from which to launch the inevitable assault on the continent. We didn't know when it was coming, and we didn't know who was going.

One night in early June I was at a dance. The young British ladies were lovely and we had many opportunities to meet at dances. An announcement on the loud speaker was summoning the officers and enlisted men of several companies to report to their stations. That was it. Just like that history started to happen. The night of June 5th, 1944 I couldn't sleep all night. I heard the sound of trucks, jeeps, half-tracks and the rumbling of tanks on the roads. Planes were droning overhead. I knew the long-awaited landing in Normandy was at hand. It could have been Calais. After all, the shortest distance from England to France was from Dover to Calais. The Germans were expecting the main thrust would be at Calais, with Normandy just a diversion. They had deployed their Panzer divisions at Calais. Erwin Rommel had left his defensive position in Normandy to visit his wife. The weather was awful. It was raining heavily, and the Germans were not expecting an attack until the weather cleared up. Just try to imagine the trepidation that permeated the thoughts and minds of the many thousands of Americans, Britons, and Canadians who were about to set out for their unknown fate.

We continued to train replacements for the next few weeks. Joe Louis visited us and treated the men to several rounds of sparring. The brown bomber was indisputably the greatest heavyweight champion of the world up until that time. I had started driving an ambulance, and when the call came for us to cross the channel, and set up the first replacement depot on Normandy beach, I was still driving the ambulance, which had a wide wheel base like a Hummer. I was a corporal when I started driving the ambulance. The t/o (table of organization) called for a driver to be a sergeant. Instead of getting an extra stripe I was busted down to a buck private. The drop in grade was stated as without prejudice. I thought it was strictly prejudice. Anyway, I really didn't care. They called me "Barney Oldfield," who was the legendary race-car driver. I was a daring driver who took chances when I was called to pick someone up.

In early July we embarked for France. The channel was choppy and rough. When we approached the French coast it was getting dark. We had to wait until the next morning to land. I was on a small landing craft that was bobbing up and down all night. I slept on the canvas top of the cab, covered with a blanket. When I awoke in the morning It was raining and I was soaked. I drove my ambulance onto a ramp that was constructed to accommodate all wheeled traffic, and rolled ashore, officially joining the forces who were striving to liberate France and defeat the German aggressor. I drove through Isigny and Ste Mere Eglise. I can still see Red Buttons hanging from the church steeple when his parachute got caught. The scene is in the movie, " The Longest Day" with John Wayne and a host of well-known actors playing cameo roles.

When we landed the front line was 10 miles inland. It was then safe for the 23rd Replacement Depot to set up on the beach. We dug in with deep holes that allowed us to put folding cots there. Our role was essentially the same as in England. We trained replacements by taking them to the firing range, ten-mile hikes, etc. Captain Brandon was the chief medical officer. One night I assisted him in an emergency operation. You couldn't have pictured a more dramatic scene if it was produced in Hollywood. A pyramidal tent was set up with a bare bulb offering the only light for Dr. Brandon's surgical effort. I was standing over the patient holding a flashlight. It was an abcessed buttock that caused me to bow out before Dr. Brandon finished his work.

On the Beach

One day I had to drive to the first Allied hospital on the Normandy coast. It was close to Cherbourg. I was sitting in the cab of the ambulance reading Shakespeare's "As you Like it," I noticed a group of brass walking toward me. My heart surged as I recognized the Supreme Commander of all the Allied Forces, General Dwight David Eisenhower. I jumped down and stood at attention in front of my vehicle. Boy was he handsome in that familiar jacket, which was later named for him.

As Ike passed by I saluted him. He returned the salute and then extended his hand, and said,

"Hello Red!"

I shook his hand as the entourage with him looked on in disbelief. It was a moment that I will enjoy for the rest of my life. He became the head of SHAEF (Supreme Head of Allied Expeditionary Force) President of Columbia University, and then was a popular President of the United States for two terms. This incident grew in importance for me as he climbed the ladder of success and fame to the position of the most powerful man in the world.

The 2,000 Plane air Raid

When we set up on the beach, the debris of our attack was still there. As I walked the beach and viewed the deep craters that were made by our 16-inch Navy guns, there were still some bodies and body parts lying there. The destroyed pill boxes of the German defenders were abandoned in a hurry and many personal effects of the soldiers like letters, post cards, pictures, etc. were still there. The weather in Normandy in July and August was beautiful. That is why the French people leave the city of Paris in the summer and go to Normandy. Each day was a carbon copy of the one before it. The mornings were clear and cool, the afternoons were sunny and warm, and the evenings and nights were cool and comfortable.

Our front line troops were stalled about 15 miles from the Normandy coast at a town called St. Lo. The Air Force was called on to bomb the area and allow our armies to break through the German resistance and move east to Paris. One morning the air was filled with bombers. Every available Allied plane was pressed into service. I sat on a chair and counted hundreds of planes. It turned out that more than 2,000 planes took part in the exercise to break through the resistance at St. Lo. The raid and its aftermath ironically provided more defensive positions for the Germans. The concrete rubble was difficult to pass. It wasn't too long after the raid that our forces broke through and started their advance across northern France. All the while we were sending a steady stream of replacements to bring attacking divisions up to strength. There were many killed and wounded as the attacks grew in intensity.

After a few weeks in France, with an overwhelming amount of supplies, equipment, and personnel arriving every day, it had to become apparent to the Germans that it was only a matter of time before the war would be over. The invincible German war machine was doomed to defeat.

The Paris Escapade

It happens in civilian life all the time. Your boss asks you to train a new employee with the firm. In time your suspicions are realized. You have trained someone to take your job. Well, it happened in August, 1944 that I was sent to run a dispensary in Liege, Belgium. I worked for a replacement depot, and inevitably I became a replacement.

I didn't go directly to this new assignment, but I left the beach in a command car, which usually transported a high-ranking officer. The result was that everyone we passed automatically saluted this buck private who was riding in this command car all by himself. Hundreds of salutes gave me a sore arm, but there was a feeling of power, riding in style to join the new detachment in Compiegne, France. This was the town where the peace documents were signed in a railroad car for World War I. It was also the place where an attempt was made to kill Hitler by dissident generals.

I was billeted in a small house with about seven other men in a large room. We all had a bedroll which we rolled up every morning. We weren't there for very long, but Moishe Weiner and I became very upset because the food we were getting was inadequate. I don't know whose idea it was, but before we knew it, we were on the road trying to get a lift into Paris. If we were going to die, we might as well have a little fun while we can. It didn't take long for us to get a ride with a charcoal-burning truck. A few hours later we were walking around in the streets of Paris. We were hungry, and we didn't have a room. After trying to get a room in a hotel, it dawned on us that you couldn't get one without a pass. We could buy a loaf of bread and a bottle of wine, but I was beginning to realize that we were in trouble.

My knowledge of French was helpful, but without a pass the concierge of the hotels we entered refused to give us a room. Not only that, but the hotels notified the M.P.'s when soldiers without a pass were inquiring about a room. Finally, the inevitable happened. One hotel must have called the military police. Before we could leave, two M.P.'s, a Briton and an American confronted Moishe and I and asked for our credentials.

"Where are your passes?" they asked.

"You got me," I replied. I didn't believe in stalling. They had me dead to rights, and I was ready to face the consequences of my actions.

Meanwhile, Moishe Weiner started fumbling through his wallet and could only come up with some old laundry ticket from a Chinese laundry for a few shirts.

"I have no pass," said Moishe.

"O.K.," they said.

"Follow us."

We were marched out of the hotel and taken to the Paris Stockade, where we stayed overnight before returning to our outfit. There were no beds. We had to sleep on a concrete floor, and it was cold. There was no steam. A small stove was in the center of the big room, and we slept close to the stove and tried to keep warm.

The next morning it was obvious that we weren't the only ones who were caught. In fact, a whole railway battalion, including the commanding officer and his aides were caught selling whole railroad cars loaded with food, gasoline, cigarettes, perfume, nylons, liquor, etc. The officers and men were kept in isolation because they were worried that the soldiers in the stockade would do them harm. It was made known that General George S. Patton's tanks were stopped because there was a shortage of fuel. This was selling gasoline on the black market and interfering with our ability to win the war.

I also met an old friend who went through basic training with me. He was caught selling all kinds of merchandise on the black market. He explained to me why he was doing it.

"Hey Red, I might get five years in the stockade. Not only will I be safe until the war is over, but when I get out, I'll be rich and never have to work for the rest of my life. I own two hotels, a brothel, and I have stashed away enough gold, diamonds, and other jewelry in banks all over Paris. I have a couple of partners who will watch things until I get out."

"You got it all figured out." I said.

"Yeah, I have nothing to worry about," he replied.

As for me, I had plenty to worry about. My partner and I were sent to an outdoor camp near Etampes, about 20 miles outside of Paris. We had to live in pup tents and it was snowing, and it was very cold. The only diversion was the entertainment supplied by the prostitutes who commuted from Paris. They were busy, while Moishe and I sat on a hill and watched them ply their trade. The pimp passed among us and asked,

"Zig-zig?"

"Non, spectator, compris spectator?"

The next day we were put on a train that took 24 hours to go only 25 miles. We reached our company and were ushered in to see the captain.

"Do you two realize that this is wartime?" he asked.

"I could charge you both with desertion, or being AWOL(away without official leave). But I know you had no time to even see Paris."

"You will both have to spend one week doing extra duty in the kitchen!"

"You're dismissed!"

Moishe and I returned to our room and reveled in the thought that we took off because we weren't getting enough food. Now we were working in the kitchen where we could eat all we wanted. Boy, were we lucky.

We were all right now. Except that one night Moishe comes into our room, and I noticed his jacket was bulging. He unzipped his windbreaker and revealed a 25 pound turkey.

"What's wrong with you?" I said. "What are you going to do with that bird?"

"I'll cook it in the fireplace!" he replied.

"You'll do nothing of the sort. You'll burn down the whole house."

"Now, you have to figure out a way of sneaking the turkey back into the kitchen!"

It wasn't easy, but Moishe managed to get that turkey back into the freezer without being seen. All was finally well. A couple of days later the whole company was on its way to the town of Liege, Belgium. We marched through the city on the main street, to the delight of the Belgians who had recently been liberated by the American Army.

A New Life Amid the Dying

When we left the comfortable billets in Compiegne, the replacements with me were destined to follow the advancing armies as they moved toward Germany. It was no picnic. We had to pitch pup tents in the open fields. It was raining constantly and the mud was almost mid-calf deep. It was hard to walk, and the rain was pouring into my pup tent. Strange as it may seem, the prostitutes managed to set up shop in a tent, and the horny G.I.'s were lined up in the rain waiting their turn.

There was no let up. Our daily routine was beginning to get me down. The Day of Atonement came in late September, 1944, and a cantor who came from Poland conducted the service. His whole family (300) three hundred people were all killed in the concentration camps. One of the cooks was Jewish, and he managed to forage for fresh eggs. He made a feast to break the fast that was delicious. He baked a peach pie for dessert, and we had a steak with all the trimmings. It was hard to imagine that we were wallowing in the mud somewhere in Belgium, and we had such a great Yom Kippur.

My buddy and I decided to look around in the area to see if we could find a place to clean up. We were dirty, tired, and water-logged. We didn't have a good night's sleep in a long time. I thought that my knowledge of French could help us find a hospitable farmer who would put us up for the night. As luck would have it, I found a farm house where the owner was a friendly gentleman who invited us to sleep over. That's all I asked for, one night. We had hot showers and a warm bed with down pillows and comforters. It was heaven.

I fell into a deep sleep, and after a few hours I was awakened by a loud knocking at my door. I thought the Germans had come.

"Schnell, schnell!" shouted the farmer, reverting to German. (He spoke to me in French).

"O.K. what's the matter? Vas ist los?"

I followed him downstairs and he kept motioning toward the barn. When we entered, I saw a cow on her side. She was having a calf. The head was sticking out. The farmer looped a heavy rope that was tied to a wooden stick around the head. It was difficult to get the rest of the calf's body out of his mother, but we did. I experienced the feeling of creation in that exhilarating exercise. Strange things happen in strange places. This was one of those incidents that stand out in a lifetime of events. I felt that I had repaid my farmer for the hospitality he provided for me and my buddy. The war was far removed for that moment in time, but it was not lost. As we returned to our muddy bivouac area to resume the life of a soldier, it was waiting, watching, and hoping for a safe resolution of the war. We followed orders, and we were on our way to more exciting and certainly more dangerous experiences.

A Belgian Interlude

I was transferred to a medical detachment in Liege, a rather large city in Belgium. I was assigned to handle the morning sick call, which usually had about 25 to 30 soldiers reporting some minor ailment or sickness. I treated sprained ankles, colds, fevers, pneumonia, and other complaints. If I got into trouble, there was a doctor in the hospital who could diagnose the problem. It was the start of "telemedicine."

I did a very good job, and never got into any problems. During the time I was in Liege I met a lovely family with two young women. My buddy Dan Kellner and I were dating the daughters and we spent several weekends at the home of the Nizet family. They treated us to home cooking and my knowledge of French amazed and delighted them. There was a close call one day when a buzz bomb, a V1 rocket landed near the house and almost destroyed it. Fortunately, we all survived that bomb.

As winter approached, we were confident that the war would soon be over. We were at the German border, and the Russians were attacking from the east, after the battle for Stalingrad. However, Hitler had other ideas. His armored columns caught the allies by surprise and broke through the American positions in the Ardennes. Several divisions were sent on R & R just before Christmas. The hysteria and panic created by the German attack caused a call-up of every available soldier near the front. I was told that we would be leaving for the front on Christmas morning, 1944.

On Christmas Eve we were treated to a U.S.O. show. Thousands of us spent our last evening with Bob Hope, Bing Crosby, Frances Langford, and Jerry Colonna. It was another scene that I shall never forget. It was snowing, and thousands of soldiers were sitting on their helmets in a large field. They were crying, as Bing Crosby was singing White Christmas. Thoughts of home, worries about combat which they faced in the days ahead, and ultimately, the fear that they would not make it home alive. It was a touching scene, that I'm sure all the survivors will never forget.

The Malmedy Massacre

When I joined C Company, the 26th Regiment of the First Infantry Division, I had no idea where we were located. The position was in the Ardennes Forest in Belgium. It was close to the German border. No one discussed the geographical area we were defending. I do remember seeing a sign on the road which indicated the direction to Butgenbach and St. Vith. Those two towns were the closest to us. Bastogne was a few miles south of our position. The junction of St. Vith was an important crossroad which we had captured and stopped the advance of the German panzer divisions. I didn't know it when I was on the line, and I doubt if any soldiers in my company or regiment knew the significance or importance of the battle for St. Vith. I learned about the logistics of the battle by reading several books about the Battle of the Bulge.

After tending the unfortunate Signal Corpsman who lost both legs, I had used my one tourniquet and my belt. In addition, I had used all the sulfur powder to treat the many dozens of holes caused by shrapnel. I had, in effect, emptied my whole first aid kit and its supplies. I had to leave my company in the grove of trees and walk to the field hospital to replenish my first aid equipment. The long barrage of 88 artillery shells, mortars, and machine guns had felled all the trees covering our foxholes. I filled my first aid kit with bandages, sulfur powder, band aids, a tourniquet, morphine syrettes, and started to return to my company. I was looking for the trees that marked our position. It had snowed the niht before and the whole area was blanketed with the white stuff. It was a lovely winter scene. The German attack had completely changed the look of our position. So did a foot of snow.

I was walking for half an hour through the deep snow and I was beginning to worry that I would never find my way back. I noticed several shallow holes which were the earmark of the German defensive positions. I continued walking and at least a half an hour later and more than a couple of miles, I saw a soldier standing guard in the open field. It was a relief to see an American who was guarding the perimeter of our position.

"What's the password, soldier?" he asked.

I was stunned for the moment, but relieved to hear a friendly voice, and an English-speaking soldier. Fortunately, I remembered the password, and said,

"The eagle has landed."
"What outfit are you with?"
"C Company, 26th Regiment, The Big Red One. Where are they?"
"When I left they were in a grove of trees up on a hill. The Krauts have leveled the trees and the snow has covered my position."
"You're lucky you saw me," he said.
"You were headed right into the German lines!"

"Just head back that way," he said, pointing to the place I had just come from.
"It's about 400 or 500 yards from where we are."
I was relieved to think that I escaped being captured, and that I could rejoin my company. I tucked that experience into my memory bank, and it never dawned on me that I had actually escaped more than just capture. I may have avoided death.

I didn't know it almost seventy years ago, because I never knew how close I was to the town of Malmedy. I found out recently when I found a book that was published in England that had a detailed analysis of the Battle of the Bulge and the fight for St. Vith. A map of the area graphically showed how close I was to Malmedy. My company was in the northern shoulder near Butgenbach, which was a stone's throw from Malmedy (see map). This was the site of the massacre of 86 American prisoners that the Germans had captured during the breakthrough called, "The Bulge." Twenty escaped (they were wounded) and 12 were killed by their prisoners. Hundreds of retreating Americans were rounded up by the Germans and marched into barbed wire camps. The German generals decided that prisoners of war would slow their offensive, and since they were behind schedule, they chose to eliminate the prisoners.

It is a bitter lesson of history, that tragically is lost on some members of congress, who dwell on the niceties of the Geneva Convention, and the rights of the detainees in Guantanamo Bay, Cuba, or the treatment of the prisoners in Iraq. In a war for survival, which we are fighting, there is no time for holding hands with our dangerous enemy who is determined to kill us. Cutting off heads is not the way Americans do things. Our enemy has a tradition of decapitating his adversary. We must get tough, or we will end up second best.

I realize now, looking at that map, if I had been captured by the Germans, I might very well have been part of that Malmedy massacre. I'm sure that many other unreported killings of prisoners took place. The Malmedy massacre is graphically depicted in the movie, "The Battle of the Bulge," with Henry Fonda, Dana Andrews, Telly Savalas, and Charles Bronson. The prisoners were trucked to an open field, the flaps at the back of the trucks were lifted, and the machine guns mowed down everyone. It is one of the most despicable acts perpetrated by the Germans in World War II

Frostbite

While I slept for 21 hours, the Germans bombarded our position with a steady barrage of 88 artillery shells, Schmeisser Machine Pistols, and mortar shells. When I awoke and crawled out of my foxhole it was dark. I had no idea how long I was out. Most of the men in my company stayed in their foxholes and tried to avoid getting hit. Anything else would be disastrous. A direct hit or near the hole was a ticket to heaven. When the deafening attack let up I walked around and checked with some of the men around me. One guy came up to me and said,

"Hey doc, I have a headache. Do you have an asoirin?"

"Go back to your hole," I said. Are you kidding? Men are dying around here. I have no aspirin. Just be happy you didn't get hit!"

I made the rounds and made sure no one was wounded. Some men were complaining that their feet were frozen, and it was hard for them to walk. I sent them back to the forward aid station, and tagged them with frostbite. As I walked around, I noticed that my legs were heavy. It felt like I was lifting sacks of cement with each step I took. It dawned on me that I might have frostbite myself. I took off my boots and noticed that all ten toes were swollen and dark blue. It didn't take long for me to realize that I couldn't walk anymore. I had to drag my feet to move a few yards. I couldn't last much longer in that condition and I wasn't able to do my job. I dragged myself to the forward aid station and tagged myself with frostbite. I laid down on a stretcher.

A medical officer walked into the room while I was waiting to be evacuated, and he ordered me to put my feet in a large pot of very hot water. I protested.

"Sir," I said, "that is just the wrong thing to do. I am a medic, and I know that hot water will make my toes swell up and itch. I respectfully request that you don't make me do it!"

"Soldier! that's an order!' he said officiously. With that he walked away and I never saw him again.

After an hour of soaking my toes in hot water, I took my feet out of the pot, dried them thoroughly, and put cotton between each toe. As I predicted, the toes got so swollen that I could no longer fit them in my shoes. Then they started to change color. Within a couple of hours they were all completely black. There was no feeling in them at all. They were numb, and the blood was frozen in all ten toes. I couldn't feel a thing.

Just then a soldier passed by my stretcher and placed a beautiful new pair of fur-lined boots at my feet. What timing! Maybe if I had received those boots two weeks before, I would still be on the line attending to my company's medical needs. After a while, an ambulance pulled up and I was lifted into it by a couple of men. As we started rolling away from the front lines I was looking up at the ceiling of the ambulance, and thinking that my destiny was to survive. The prognosis of my feet was still unclear, and I didn't know whether I could save my toes, but I was certain that I would live. The front was dangerous. There were no life insurance salesmen selling policies to the men in their foxholes. The ambulance drove me to a railroad station where the wounded were loaded onto stretchers in specially built cars that held them against the walls. The train was packed with men from General George S. Patton's Sixth Armored Division who were fighting in Bastogne. They had broken legs, arms, and various other wounds. Some were blind, and it was a hectic scene. The whole group of wounded were headed for a general hospital in Paris.

It wasn't possible for my frostbitten toes to get any blacker. They were very black. There was no feeling. They were numb and achy. I was only in Paris for a couple of days, and my knowledge of French was helpful; in communicating with the nurses. One day a nurse came over to my bed with a clipboard and a pen. She asked me to sign at the bottom of the paper.

"Quest-ce Que Ce?"

"You must sign and give permission to amputate your toes!"

"Are you crazy?" "Etes-vous fou?" I answered

"If you cut off my big toe I"ll have to limp for the rest of my life!"

"No, thank you. I'll take my chances that my toes will heal." I didn't sign.

In retrospect I was taking a big risk in allowing for the possibility of the spread of my problem, and the potential for gangrene. That might have necessitated the amputation of part of my legs. It was a very difficult decision for a twenty year old to make. There was no way of knowing how things would turn out. Many men just went along with the doctors and had several toes amputated. Who knows if I did the right thing.

The 12th General Hospital in England

A few days later I was taken to an airport where a DC2 airplane was specially equipped to transport wounded soldiers on litters. We were flown over the English Channel and landed in the British midlands. The final destination was the 12th General Hospital near Leamington Spa. This was to be my home for almost ninety (90) days. It was not a picnic. My ward was filled with men who had frostbite, and many of them had their toes amputated. It was February, 1945. The doctors had no idea what to do for frostbite. They didn't know how to treat it. We were given three shots of whiskey (Spiritus Frumenti) every day, one before each meal. This was supposed to improve your circulation. Another treatment was Buerger's exercises. We lifted our legs overhead and then lowered them over the side of the bed. Then we put our feet in a solution of water and potassium permanganate. It was a purple liquid that was used to help the healing process. The truth is that the process of healing had its own timetable. It was a slow, painful , progression that couldn't be hurried. I couldn't walk for ninety days, and even then I had to use a cane for support. There were some men who enjoyed the whiskey. They lined up for drinks as often as they could, but I couldn't drink that stuff.

It was impossible to sleep, and it was necessary to keep your feet outside of the blanket. There was more than a month of thawing out. The pain was intense, and I don't remember getting any medication to ease the pain. Maybe they gave us an aspirin. In the morning my feet were wet from thawing out and sweating. In time all my toenails fell off, and the tissues of all the toes peeled off. The toes were very tender and raw. It was the most difficult period of my recuperation. I spent my time during the days and weeks I was in the hospital writing letters and reading.

Some of the men around me were interesting, and one in particular had a fabulous family history. His name was Ogletree. He lived in Georgia. He told me that his great grandfather was a traitor to the rebel cause during the Civil War. He was General George Winfield Scott, Abraham Lincoln's Commanding General of the Union Armies. Think of it! A Southerner, the head of all the Union armies. Ogletree's whole family would not talk to him.

It was important to look for diversions to take your mind off the difficult period of healing. As time passed, the tissues of my toes began to heal and the nails began to grow back. Eventually, they were fully grown, and back to normal.

When I was able to walk again, I started to visit the various wards around the hospital. At first, I borrowed a guitar and entertained the bedridden men who had serious wounds in the traction ward. They had broken arms and legs and were locked into position. They couldn't move. I also wrote articles for the Stars and Stripes, a newspaper that was distributed to the Armed Services. I wrote about celebrities who had earned the Purple Heart, Bronze Star, Silver Star, etc. Several major league baseball players were in the 12th General Hospital. When I visited the wards I asked the men what they needed. They hadn't been paid in months, and since they were wounded in combat, they didn't have time to shop or acquire the necessities of life. They needed razors, blades, combs, cigarettes, toothpaste, toothbrushes, candy, gum, etc. These items were not the most important things one needs, maybe trivial to some, but they were necessary. I knew the Red Cross Club at the hospital had closets full of those items. I just made a list and presented it to the Red Cross women at the club. Well, you might learn why so many soldiers and veterans are not fans of the Red Cross. I looked in the closets and saw all the things that the men wanted. I knew they were there. When I asked if I could distribute the various items to the men, I was told,

"I can't give you any of these things!"

"Why?" I asked.

"Well, we don't know how long the war is going to last and there is no way of knowing if we are going to get any more of these things."

I was furious, and I didn't make a secret of my feelings. How could they refuse to give these wounded soldiers the things they needed. That is why Americans donate money to the Red Cross.

The next day I raided the Red Cross club with a laundry bag, and cleaned out the closet. Santa Claus then visited the traction ward and gave the men the things they wanted. It was one of the most soul-satisfying moments of my stay in that hospital. Another thing that I loved, and almost brought tears to my eyes was watching the young English girls who visited the hospital to read the mail to the blind soldiers. It was heart-warming to see how happy they were to hear from home. Those girls were doing a worthy thing. Someone had to do it, and they were great to volunteer for this difficult job.

A Kosher Meal

My ten-day stay in London was eventful and interesting. In addition to the sightseeing, I was able to see a musical called, "Panama Hattie" with Bebe Daniels and Ben Lyon. I had learned of a kosher delicatessen called Bloom's in Aldgate, on the East end of London. I thought it would be a good idea to eat a kosher hot corned beef or pastrami sandwich. After all, it was more than two years since I had enjoyed such a meal.

I was standing at a bus stop, waiting to catch the red, double-decker bus to Whitechapel. On the queue, next to me were a young woman and her mother. I noticed that the young woman was wearing a necklace with the Star of David. This demonstrated that she was Jewish. I asked her,

"Could you tell me where I can get a good, hot pastrami sandwich?" Is this the bus to Whitechapel?"

The mother immediately chimed in and said,

"You don't have to worry. Just come with us and we will see that you are treated to a good kosher meal."

As it turned out, we ended up on the East End of London, which was the equivalent of the Lower East Side of New York. We climbed upstairs in an old building, and to my surprise I was ushered in to a typical Jewish wedding. If I closed my eyes, I would think I was back in New York on Delancey Street. The British people surrounded me and fawned all over me. They gave me a bottle of scotch and the young, eligible girls were seated at my table. It wasn't lost on me that there was an attempt on their part to sort of hope that I would take a shine to one of the girls.

The meal was a traditional meal that you would expect on a Friday evening. It started with chicken soup and chopped liver, and the main course was roast chicken, stuffed derma and vegetables. I was at home. What is most important, I felt at home and comfortable. The war was forgotten. Here I was, enjoying a delicious meal, the music was playing, and I was surrounded by nice people who were showing their appreciation for a "Yank" who was doing his best to defeat an enemy that had almost destroyed their country. It was a soul-satisfying experience that I shall never forget.

The family that brought me to the wedding invited me to their home for the week-end. They lived in Luton, which was about 30 miles from London. In retrospect, they might have thought that a couple of days at their home would create some chemistry between me and their daughter. Nothing like that happened. It was just a fine gesture on the part of a British family to host an American. I returned to London and in a few days I was on my way back to the continent to resume my duties. The war was winding down, but there was no way of knowing how long it would last.

Victory in Europe

When I was released from the hospital, I was assigned to limited duty because of my disability. I had to report to the Headquarters company of the 31st AAA (Anti-Aircraft Artillery) Battalion. It was attached to the 9th Air force. However, I was given a 10-day delay en route, which gave me enough time to spend a week in London. This was my first visit to this great city, which withstood the "Blitz" and survived due to a great leader, Winston Churchill, and a gritty people with a "never say die" spirit. They faced this air assault all alone, as the world watched in horror.

The "whispering gallery" at St. Paul's Cathedral gave me a bird's eye view of the devastation caused by German bombers. Wide areas of central London were destroyed. I saw the usual tourist sites-Big Ben, Trafalgar Square, The Tate Gallery, Piccadilly Circus, the Tower Bridge, Westminster Abbey, and The Houses of Parliament, Covent Garden, and many others.

A moment of history happened while I was having doughnuts and coffee in a Red Cross Club. It was April 12, 1945. A Red Cross woman stepped up to the microphone and said,g   "May I have your attention, please?" The assembled group of servicemen stopped their conversation and listened attentively while the woman continued.

"I have an important announcement to make," she said. With that she started to choke up and cry. She was unable to talk for a few minutes. When she finally composed herself and was able to talk, she went on—

"This morning, April 12, 1945, President Franklin Delano Roosevelt passed away." The hush that preceded the news was followed by a grieving audience, who realized that their commander-in-chief had died. He was in poor health, and it was a shame that he couldn't live to see the end of the war and the victory that he was so confident would happen. Grown men, hardened by a war that had matured young boys overnight by their death-defying experiences cried, for their leader was no longer there to give them the support they needed to continue the fight.

There was little time to mourn the passing of our leader. We had a job to do. The war had to be won, and I was on my way to the continent to join the 31st AAA Battalion which was stationed in Namur, Belgium. This outfit had been fighting overseas for more than two years, starting in North Africa, Sicily, Italy, and then up in the European theatre in Normandy. They were slated to go home as soon as the hostilities were over. That is what the men were told. The war ended in Europe on May 7, 1945. We all celebrated the victory and looked forward to the day when we could go home and join our families and loved ones. We just wanted to resume our lives.

I remember the day that General Chapin called us together to make an announcement of our departure.

"Gentlemen," he said," "this is the Army." (we were actually part of the Air Force)

"We follow orders and do what our superiors tell us to do."

I was beginning to feel uneasy by this introduction to his statement. It didn't sound encouraging.

"We are going to Germany to be part of the Army of Occupation. We leave for Langenselbold, Germany (near Frankfurt) next week."

I don't have to tell you how crushed the men were. We went out to a bar and began to drink our sorrow away. We ordered cognac and beer, and every one of us was so drunk we couldn't see straight. Bob Balger, a buddy of mine told me he was O.K., but I saw him in the men's room, on the floor, straddling the commode, and draped over it. We were very upset, and the drinking didn't change anything. We were going to Germany.

Non-Fraternization

As we rolled into Langenselbold, Germany to establish our presence with the occupation forces, it became perfectly clear that we must isolate ourselves from the German villagers. Langenselbold was seventeen kilometers from Frankfurt-am-Main. We were assigned to a castle that was once the home of a baron. The officers were in the main building, and the enlisted men were assigned to small houses that were originally the servants' quarters. These apartments were at the edge of the property. The windows looked out on a twenty foot drop down a grassy hill.

The initial policy of the Army was non-fraternization. The whole complex, including the castle was surrounded by barbed wire. The difficulty of preserving this policy was immediately obvious. There was no way that you could keep young men with raging hormones away from pretty, young, love-starved German women. They brought ladders and climbed into the windows of our rooms. But that was not usually what happened. The men would roll up a blanket and climb down the ladders. It was not unusual to see ten or twenty couples on the blankets, doing what comes naturally. Of course, there were no lights, so the darkness offered the men the anonymity they needed to continue their physically erotic exercise.

The castle was busy too. There were officers and Red Cross women who didn't have to resort to blankets in the grass, or the mosquitoes which swarmed around the men on the warm summer nights. The happy hours preceding dinner led to many happy hours after dinner. When it became obvious that the policy of non-fraternization was unworkable, the rules were changed and we were then allowed to mingle with the townspeople. At the beginning there were only displaced persons working in the compound. Eventually, the Germans were allowed to be part of the scene. They worked in the kitchen. We had a German barber, and the villagers performed other household duties in and around the castle.

My Occupation Duties

The first job I had in Germany was running a 12-drop switchboard. I liked that duty because I was on for 12 hours and then I had 24 hours off. It gave me more time to pursue my interests. We had a softball team, and I had progressed to the point where I could play at about 100 percent of my potential. I had come a long way from my condition in Namur, Belgium, when I had joined the 31st AAA Headquarters Company. A local businessman who noticed that I was limping gave me a cane to help with my balance.

The atmosphere at our base was a happy one. We had a keg of beer set up in the middle of our compound, and every soldier had a job to do. The weather was fine all through the summer, and it helped to ease the anxiety we all felt about waiting to go home.

After a while on the switchboard, I added another job. I learned how to operate a movie projector, and became a projectionist. Twice a week I would take a jeep and ride to the quartermaster depot and select a movie that I would run at night. I then set up the projector, threading the film, so that it was ready to be shown after dinner.

In addition to those duties, I set up a dispensary and was in charge of the medical needs of the company. I was the only one who had the medical experience and the first aid knowledge to handle complaints that arose. The officers saw to it that I had all the necessary equipment, and all the drugs and medications that I needed.

The Kitchen Accident

My medical duties were important to the personnel in the castle where we were privileged to be stationed during the occupation. There were the usual complaints which were easy to handle. Most of the problems that arose were small, and the people in Liege were many times the amount of those at the station in Langenselbold.

One morning, when I was on the switchboard, two of the Polish women who worked in the kitchen came running in to the office and summoned me to follow them immediately to an emergency. An accident had happened that the staff in the kitchen could not handle. As I entered the kitchen there were eight people standing in a circle watching the victim of an accident. I had them spread out and it turned out that one of the German boys who worked as a dishwasher accidentally had a sharp carving knife pierce his thigh and cut an artery. The blood was gushing out and spurting over four feet into the air. All the people were standing around and watching the life's blood of this poor boy leave his leg, and drain his energy.

My combat medic experience came in handy. The number one rule of first aid is to keep calm. I immediately put a tourniquet above the wound, and the bleeding stopped. After about ten or fifteen minutes I was able to dress the wound so that no infection would occur. After bandaging the cut, I released the pressure on the tourniquet, to make sure that the bleeding had stopped. The staff that had assembled grew in size as several of the officers and men rushed in to see what had happened.

When I finished, I received a round of applause from the audience. It was the first time I ever had that kind of accolade for just doing my duty. On the front line there was no audience, and no applause. I just did my job, packed up my first aid kit, and returned to my foxhole.

How to Build a Dance Hall

Once fraternization was permitted, it dawned on the commanding officer that we would need a social hall to cater to the needs of the men. It was decided to build a social hall, complete with a stage, and one that was large enough to have dances and variety shows.

How does one go about it? Well, it took only one week to build. We sent out several trucks. They pulled up at a few lumber yards and requisitioned all the necessary lumber. More than one hundred men were trucked in from the displaced persons camp. They worked unusually fast because they were told that when the hall was completed, they would be allowed to join in the events that were to be held.

The excitement was obvious, as the social hall took shape. When it was finished, it became the center of all the activity that we enjoyed every evening. Twice a week we had dances. Truckloads of young women were brought in from the displaced persons camp at Landsberg. Some of the women from Russia, Estonia, Lithuania, Hungary, and Romania were beautiful. They were also starved for companionship, attention, and love. I must admit that there was one particular woman that interested me. There was only one problem. She was married and reluctant to offer herself to anyone. However, she was pleasant company, and it was a rewarding experience for both of us. It must have been good, if it had such a lasting effect on me.

We left the dance hall with a jeep. Her name was Endla. A friend of mine took his girl, and I took Endla. We stopped about a mile away. My buddy had his way with his partner, but I must admit that my reluctant friend could only remind me that she was married and could not be unfaithful to her husband. It was unclear to me where her husband was at that time. Lives were so upset during the war, that families had no idea where their loved ones were sent. I was understanding, and was content to be in the company of such a lovely woman. I never saw her again.

Drying up Hoy

Irwin Hoy, from Ames, Iowa, was my roommate in Germany. We shared a small room with two beds, a window, and a restroom. He was a tall, handsome soldier with blond hair. He was also our cook. He made the greatest pancakes you could ever eat. They were high and fluffy and delicious. You didn't need a knife to cut them, you could just use a fork. He claimed the secret was using lard.

Irwin was a ladies' man who was the most well-endowed guy I ever met. He loved his sex, and didn't care where he got it. He was stationed in Marseille, France for several months and had many girl friends. One was so madly in love with him that she traveled over one thousand miles through check points and barbed wire fences, just to get to once more be in the arms of this well-hung lover. I didn't mind being in the same room with Irwin. He brought women in now and then, but he had to get up at 4 o'clock to go to work in the kitchen.

One morning I was awakened with the noise of a squishing sound. Irwin was shaking the contents of a bottle of "Eau de Pinaud" which is an after-shave lotion) onto his penis. I rose to confront him, and asked,

"What are you doing?"

"It kills it," he said.

"What are you talking about?" "What kills it?"

"Strip it down!" I said.

The short arm inspection proved positive. He stripped his long member and a white, creamy, substance oozed out of it.

"You son-of-a-bitch. You have a dose. You have Gonorrhea!" "I warned you to be careful with these oversexed and desperate German women." "Now you've done it."

"How is it going to look for our cook, who makes our food and serves it to us, has a sexually transmitted disease?"

"Who is going to want to eat your food?"

"Please, Red, help me. Can you do something to cure it?"

I realized that it would be a disaster if the brass knew about Hoy's condition. How could we allow a cook with gonorrhea serving our soldiers? I told him to keep our secret while I tried to dry up his condition. I had sulfadiazine and sulfathiazole pills in my dispensary. I started Hoy on 2 pills every 4 hours and warned hin to drink a lot of water. It worked like a charm. Within 48 hours he was completely cured of his dose. No one either then or now ever knew of his dilemma, and he was very happy and appreciative. We were great friends for the five or six months that I was in Germany. I haven't seen Hoy since 1945.

The German Funeral

Rudolph was a barber. From the first time I met him he tried to be friendly. He actually offered to give me a haircut every day! Ridiculous! However, we had a good relationship, even though he claimed that "he never saw a Nazi." Rudy had a small motorcycle which was our means of transportation when our time off allowed it. I could have disassembled the motorcycle and mailed it home for only 37 dollars.

One day we were driving through the countryside and were forced to stop alongside the narrow road. In the distance I could hear music , and I could see a large group of people approaching. They were marching about eight abreast, and slowly made their way past Rudolph and I. It turned out that this was a German funeral, as it is traditionally done in small country towns. The Burgomeister (mayor) and his aides led the parade. They were all wearing tuxedoes (World War I vintage) and then over one hundred people, with the family in front and the rest of the town behind them.

A large 25 piece band followed the crowd and was playing a funeral dirge. The horse-drawn hearse carrying the deceased had windows on both sides and draped Austrian shades. It was a scene that will forever remain in my memory. The townspeople in the rural areas of Germany, continued to do things the traditional way. The war could not change the way people had honored the memory of their dead for hundreds of years. Rudy and I waited until the funeral procession was well past us, before we mounted the motorcycle and went on our way.

The U.S.O. Troupe

When Shirley Robinson and Abe Cohen walked into our mess hall, there was a fork on the floor. I noticed the pert, little, redhead. She was cute, and I wanted to get to know her. I said,

"Look out, there's a fork in the road!"

Shirley sat down to dinner and I found out that she played the accordion. Abe Cohen was a short, pudgy, comedian who had a hilarious routine that was right out of vaudeville. The guys loved him. This was the start of a lasting friendship with Shirley. The U.S.O. Troupe was stationed in Hanau, which was about five miles away from my base in Langenselbold. I saw as many shows as I could when I had time away from my duties. Hanau was a large air base.

Shirley was a determined young lady who was afraid of nothing. She insisted that I have dinner with her in the Officers' mess one day. As an enlisted man I was prohibited from eating with the officers. However, I was her guest, and nothing was said, and I was able to dine with her in the officers' dining hall. We attended a football game in Frankfurt and Shirley's red hair and comely appearance attracted the attention of all the people around us. They probably were thinking, "Who is that buck private with that lovely woman?"

The affair with Shirley Robinson lasted for months. It was a wartime romance that comes and goes as events bring people together and then pull them apart. When I had to leave for home, we said our good-byes, and no promises of any kind were exchanged.

Almost Raped

It was no secret that the German women in the town were love-starved. Their men were fighting all over Europe for more than ten years. They were without sex and the companionship of their husbands and boyfriends all that time, and it obviously had an effect on them. We were wary and cautious about dealing with the German townspeople.

One day I was walking through the town at dusk. I was all alone. All of a sudden, a young woman jumped out of the shadows and grabbed me firmly in her arms. She started to kiss me furiously. She began to grope me all over and eventually reached into my pants and wanted to grab my genitals. I was aroused and almost willing to submit to this sexual attack. I couldn't see my assailant, but she was a large woman that was very strong.

I had no shortage of female companions in the town, and this was not my idea of sexual enjoyment. Wrestling with a woman in an alley, with all my clothes on, and having to fight her off, was definitely not on my mind. I caught a look at her face, and she wasn't exactly Hedy Lamarr. The whole encounter took ten or fifteen minutes. She finally relaxed her grip on me and was willing to accept my wishes. If I was interested in continuing this situation with her, I could have done so. She offered to take me to her house, where ostensibly, we would be alone and could continue the love-making in a more normal manner. I declined her invitation and sent her on her way. I really didn't know what she looked like. I didn't know her name, and I never saw anyone who resembled her for all the months that I spent in the town. It was an experience that I will always remember. It demonstrates the strength and power of the sexual urge. I was the object of the attack because I just happened to be at that place at that time. It could have happened to anyone.

General's Mess

For over one month I was a waiter for the six highest ranking officers of the company. I served General Chapin, Colonel Moore, a lieutenant colonel, and three majors. It wasn't a difficult job, and I was able to eat the fabulous food that general's mess provided. The enlisted men had great food, but the general and his twenty-two officers had superlative quality fare. They also had their own chef who prepared the best and most delicious meals.

When I left the front lines I weighed 155 pounds. After the hospital, Belgium, and Germany, I billowed up to 180 pounds. General's mess in Frankfurt supplied the highest quality steaks, chops, fish, lobster, and other delicacies.

Our chef supplied homemade pies, cakes, and freshly made ice cream. I made the ice cream in a wooden bucket. It was simple. You poured cream, sugar, peaches, and ice onto the bucket, and you cranked the handle until it got nice and thick. Then you put it in the freezer. It was the best. We didn't worry about cholesterol then.

This was one of the jobs that kept me busy while we all waited to be sent home. The war was still on in the Pacific, and the Japanese were desperately trying to defend the islands that the Americans were invading, as they got closer to the mainland of Japan.

A Major Throat Cure

One day I was confronted with another medical emergency. Major Conway had to deliver a speech in Frankfurt and he came up with a severe case of laryngitis. He had completely lost his voice. I had only forty-eight hours to provide a medical miracle. He appealed to me to do what I could to cure his condition.

Well, I had secretly straightened out Irwin Hoy and his problem. So, I told the major that I couldn't promise him anything, but I would try. There were no doctors around, so he was stuck with me. I told Major Conway to follow my instructions carefully. He took 2 sulfadiazene tablets every four hours and got plenty of sleep. He also had to drink at least 8 to 10 glasses of water.

For some strange reason, sulfur-based medications work very well with some people. They did with the good major. Within twenty-four hours he was as good as ever. His voice came back completely. He was able to deliver his speech in Frankfurt, and my cure was the talk of the castle. All the officers, including General Chapin congratulated me on the great job I did for the major. For me, it was all in a day's work.

Frankfurt Synagogue on Passover

More than nine hundred soldiers from all over Germany were invited to a Passover Seder. The Jewish Welfare Board arranged the whole thing, and gave us boxes of matzoh and other goodies. We gathered together, soldiers of the Hebrew faith, to continue a multi-century tradition. It was particularly fitting to have the Seder in the largest synagogue in Europe. The Frankfurt Synagogue had the roof blown out by the Germans and the large front doors were sealed until the war was over.

It was a touching scene. There were Jewish boys from all over Germany, Belgium, and France joining a ceremony that their fathers and grandfathers celebrated to commemorate the exodus from Egypt and the slavery of their ancestors. It is a ritual that thanks God for "taking his children out of bondage with a strong hand and an outstretched arm."

The celebration in Frankfurt, in its own way, was a celebration of the victory over a tyrant who wanted to enslave the whole world. It was not lost on the assembly that over 13 million people were killed by Hitler, and 6 million Jews from all over Europe were exterminated in the Holocaust. All in all, it was a very happy day, we were free, and we were going home.

A Furlough to Paris

I don't know if it was a reward for curing Major Conway's laryngitis, but I was granted a ten-day furlough soon after the event. I immediately made plans to go to Paris. This time I had a legitimate pass, and would have no trouble arranging for a room, while I took in the sights.

When the day arrived for my departure, I hitched a ride into Frankfurt, where I was catching a train for an overnight ride into Paris. The station was buzzing with activity. People were traveling everywhere, and Frankfurt was the hub. It wasn't long before I found out that I couldn't get a ticket to Paris. All the seats were sold out, and I was told that I would have to come back the next day and try again. How aggravating was it to spend your furlough in Germany. Time was precious. I was furious, but I didn't know what to do. Where does one go? What could I do? I'd have to rent a room in a hotel and try to arrange for a ticket on the next day.

I walked around the busy train station in a daze. Some of the pleasure of my vacation was drained out of me. I thought of returning to my base and starting all over again. It was frustrating. Just about the time I was ready to give up I passed an office which had a sign" RTO" or rail transport office. I thought that it would be worth trying to fight the red tape and if I could get to see the guy in charge, I might prevail upon him to get me a ticket, so that I could start my furlough without delay.

I walked into the RTO office and it was a microcosm of what was happening in the station. It was active and everybody was scurrying around trying to look busy. I asked someone at the front desk if I could see the rail transport officer. At that moment, a sergeant who had an armband with RTO on it to identify his position was walking toward me. My heart skipped a beat because this soldier looked familiar.

"Red! What are you doing here?" asked the sergeant.

"Chubby Kastin! You son-of-a-gun," I shouted, "I'm on a ten day furlough, and I need a ticket to Paris," I said pleadingly. We hugged each other just like long lost brothers. Chubby and I lived around the corner from each other in Brooklyn, New York. We played softball in the school yard of P.S. 101 in Bensonhurst. It was a touch of home, seeing each other.

"Your troubles are over, " Chubby said.

I'm the officer in charge here, and I have the final word on who gets out of here on all the trains.

"I'm giving you a private rail car."

"Do you want a couple of women to keep you company?" he asked.

I was speechless. What a turnaround. I had just gone from despair to elation. Chubby Kastin was very busy. He made the arrangements for me to have a private car all the way into Paris. I had female company, which was pleasant, and I arrived in Paris the next day and enjoyed myself for nine days. During my stay I met about eight people I knew including a cousin on the Champs-Elysee. I saw the usual tourist attractions including the Eiffel Tower, The Sorbonne, Pigalle, Montmartre, the Opera House, Luxemberg Gardens, the left bank, etc. It was a delightful nine days, and thanks to Chubby Kastin, my vacation was not ruined. I have not seen Chubby since that day in 1945, but fate stepped in and I'll be forever grateful that I met him in Frankfurt when a friend needed a friend.

My Nuremberg Trial

It took about five months, until September 1945, for the United States Army to come up with a program to send troops home. Until then, I was not homesick, but I must admit that I thought of home and my family very often. The total number to qualify for separation was 73 points. It was comprised of how many months you served in the United States, how many months overseas, decorations such as the Purple Heart was 5 points. Battle stars were awarded 5 points. This included North Africa, Northern Europe, the Ardennes (Battle of the Bulge) etc. I had a total of 53 points without my four battle stars and Purple Heart. However, my records were at the First Division Headquarters, which was located in Nuremberg.

I tried in vain for about two months, with phone calls and letters to get my records sent to my base, so that I could get approval to go home. Men from the 31st AAA Company were leaving, and I was getting anxious. All I needed was the confirmation of my service with the Big Red One, and I would be on my way home. I wanted to get on with my life.

My duty at that time was for 24 hours off. I decided to take things into my own hands. The best way to get things done is to do it yourself. I was going to travel to Nuremberg and personally get my records. It was a 400 kilometer trip in a strange country, with many unknowns. However, after what I had been through, I could face anything. The prospect of getting home was what drove me to undertake this perilous journey. I could only get a trip ticket for 24 hours. The jeep was open, and the windshield wiper was broken. I had to stretch my neck and look at the road without using the windshield.

I knew that I couldn't get to Nuremberg and back on time, and that would mean that I would be AWOL. The die was cast. I was on my way. I was willing to take whatever penalty resulted from my action. I wanted to go home. I worked my way through some of the largest cities in Germany, such as Heidelberg, Stuttgart, Wurzburg, and Heilbronn. When I ran out of gas, I just pulled up to any Army installation. They were happy to fill up the jeep with gas. If I wanted to have coffee and doughnuts, I stopped at a Red Cross Club. I slept over at one base. I kept my eye on the goal. I had to reach Nuremberg.

When I drove through Stuttgart, the potholes and craters in the road that were the result of our bombing made it difficult to negotiate, but I forged ahead. When I finally arrived at Nuremberg, it was just a pile of rocks. All the buildings were destroyed. There were no street signs. I managed to get to the headquarters of the First Division. I walked into the office and introduced myself. I demanded to know why they hadn't responded to my phone calls or answered my letters.

The clerk showed me a pile of correspondence about three feet high! He turned the pile over, and on the bottom were my letters. He acted promptly to cut an order for me, which represented the award of the Purple Heart and my four battle stars. I thanked him warmly, and after only about one hour, my mission was accomplished.

I started back toward Frankfurt, confident that I would now be going home. I also knew that I would have some explaining to do. The company commander would like to know why I was away without official leave. I think he would treat me kindly when he saw why I went to Nuremberg. Fortunately, my fears were unwarranted. When I showed my company commander the orders issued by the First Division, he was duly impressed.

He delivered a pro-forma lecture about the seriousness of being away without official leave (AWOL). He let me get away without extra duty. The war was over, and there was no use getting worked up about it. I was in for a big surprise. The captain showed my orders from the Big Red One to General Chapin. A few days later, the whole company was called out for a special event.

The Purple Heart Ceremony

On October 17, 1945, Headquarters Company of the 31st AAA (9th Air Force), was called out for the express purpose of presenting me with the Purple Heart. General Chapin, the colonels, a lieutenant colonel, the majors, the captains, first lieutenants, and second lieutenants, many non-commissioned officers, were standing at attention while I received my medal. It didn't occur to me at the time, but I realize it now. I was a buck private, and here was a whole company of non-commissioned officers, and officers, and a Brigadier General paying tribute to a private who earned the respect of his fellow soldiers for his service, and bestowing the honor that so many wounded men never received.

I appreciated the gesture by the general, and I was almost embarrassed by all the attention by my friends in the company. It was possible that none of the men in Headquarters Company had ever been wounded, and received the Purple Heart. It was something special for the general and all the officers and men. I was happy for the exhilarating experience, but underlying that feeling was the realization that I was now qualified to join a group of men who were going home.

A Beer in Kassel

Following my daring trip to Nuremberg, and the successful completion of my mission to get the points necessary for me to go home, I was elated. The ceremony that General Chapin put on was a bonus that I did not expect. It allowed me to experience a feeling of pride; one that many other soldiers who earned the Purple Heart could not enjoy.

An order was cut for me to join a group of men from several different bases in Germany who were going to the United States for separation from the service. I was ordered to join the other men who were assembling in Kassel, Germany, about one hundred miles to the north of Frankfurt.

It was an uneventful trip up the Autobahn, and it didn't take more than a couple of days before we were all there. I remember one night in particular, when a few of the boys spent some time in a "Steinhof." I had a stein of beer which I remember to this day. It was thick, creamy, and strong. When I finished drinking one stein, I felt great, but I was actually seeing double. It was only about 12 percent alcohol, but boy!, I remember how good it felt after drinking that one beer.

It was not too long before the whole group I was with was transferred to Munich, which was a couple of hundred miles to the south. We were ready, and we were happy, we were going home.

General George S. Patton's Fatal Accident

The trip down to Munich was quick. The Autobahn is a superlative highway which Hitler built so that his military could travel quickly throughout Germany. On the way we passed the spot that marked the untimely death of one of America's greatest generals. The driver of our car showed us the exact spot in the road where General Patton met his tragic ending. There were skid marks in the road, and it happened the day before we passed the area where it occurred.

The incident is shown in the award-winning movie, "Patton." His command car pulled out onto the Autobahn just as a truck came barreling down at a high rate of speed. It was impossible to stop. That tragic accident snuffed out the life of a successful leader. He was irascible, confrontational, and at times would disobey orders, but he will be remembered for getting the job done. He won the battle "even if it took a truckload of dog tags."

In the evening we arrived at Munich and settled down for a few days before leaving for the port of embarkation for our journey home. I was out in charge of the dispensary once again, but it only resulted in more work when we had to leave.

Munich: Where it all Started

It took several days for the group of soldiers who were headed home to arrive in Munich. The history of Munich was not lost on us. We knew that Adolph Hitler started his Nazi movement in Munich. It began with a "Putsch" in a beer hall in Munich. I was able to travel around the city until I found the place where Hitler started his movement. Americans had changed the historic place into a Red Cross Club. I was happy to have coffee and doughnuts in a place where a defeated Nazi superman had given birth to his doomed theory that Aryan supermen would take over the world.

When I came to Munich, the commanding officer of the company told me to take charge of the dispensary. I was the medic who had control of a room full of pills, drugs, and cases of condoms. We had no special duties while we were waiting for the order to continue our journey home. Our boredom was interrupted with the announcement that a U.S.O. show was coming to a theatre the night before we were to leave.

I was busy on that last day because the captain told me to get rid of the dispensary.

"I don't care what you do with the stuff. Burn it!" said the captain.

I did throw everything in the room into a pot-bellied stove and burned all the pills. I had large bottles of (1,000) aspirins, sulfadiazine, sulfathiazole, quinine, etc. I kept some stuff and carried them in my duffel bag all the way to Camp Twenty Grand or Lucky Strike in Le Havre before I got tired of carrying it. I then threw the pills away before I boarded the ship to go home.

We were all ready to go home. We packed our gear and with great anticipation we all attended the U.S.O. show at the theatre in Munich. The next morning we were on our way home.

The Final U.S.O. Show

It was my last night in Munich. I was ready to go. My duffel bag was packed with all my gear, and the excitement was building for my departure. All of my buddies were ready too. The lucky survivor of almost three years overseas and a long and painful hospital stay were history. We were going home. All the unpleasant experiences were burned into our memory and we were reveling in the thought that we would soon be on our way.

We were informed that a U.S.O. show would be our last evening's treat. There was a large theatre in Munich that hosted stage shows and concerts. It had over 700 seats. Everyone was looking forward to the show. The performers in U.S.O. shows were our bridge to home. I kept hoping that it would be my good fortune to have a reunion with my friends from Hanau. However, that was hundreds of kilometers away from Munich. It was too much to expect. It was too good to be true. I put it out of my mind. I was going home, and my cup was running over.

After dinner, a group of us left for the theatre and got settled in good orchestra seats. Hundreds of soldiers were jammed into the theatre. It was a full house. An officer took center stage and introduced the U.S.O. Troupe. My jaw dropped when I saw good old Abe Cohen and my girl friend Shirley Robinson. What an exciting night. I couldn't have asked for a better going away present than to see my friends once again. I had seen the show more than twenty times. I knew Abe Cohen's routine by heart.

"A guy goes into a restaurant and asks the waitress,
"Do you serve crabs?"
"Sit down, no one will notice you."
She walked funny, so the guy asked,
"Do you have frogs' legs?"
"No, I have rheumatism, I always walk this way."
The guy sits down and orders a cup of coffee.
He says,
"Are you sure this is coffee? It tastes like mud!"
"It was ground this morning!"
A soldier was walking down the street. A truck passed by with kegs of beer. One of the kegs rolled off and hit the soldier on the head, but it didn't hurt him.
"It was light beer!"

"I swallowed a nickel. Do notice the change in me?" Abe's routine was right out of Joe Miller's joke book. The jokes were corny, but we loved them, and the G.I's roared with delight.

When the show was over, I went backstage and had a happy reunion with Shirley and Abe. It had been a couple of months since I saw them. We all thought that we would never see each other again. I said good bye and exchanged addresses with Shirley. There were no promises made. We were aware that our friendship was a wartime romance. There was some chemistry that drew us together, while we were near each other. This was obvious when six months later Shirley called my home after she returned to the United States. Her tour was over and she was on her way home through New York. I met her in a hotel in New York City. We both realized at that meeting that our fling in Germany was great fun for both of us, but was not the kind of chemistry that could lead to a more serious relationship. We kissed good bye, and that was it. We haven't contacted one another since that last meeting in New York.

The Train to Camp Lucky Strike

It was the beginning of December, 1945. The men who had gathered in Munich were ready for the journey that would take them home. We had packed our belongings and were trucked to the railroad station to board the train that would take us to Le Havre in France. For some reason, the camps that assembled the men at Cherbourg and Le Havre were given the names of cigarettes. I was going to Camp Lucky Strike.

The railroad cars which took us to the port were the same 40 and 8 cars that the Germans used to transport the Jews, Catholics, homosexuals, gypsies, and handicapped people to Auschwitz, Dachau, Bergen-Belsen, and all the other concentration camps. Many of them were concentrated in Poland. We were crammed into the cars like so many cattle. The train was long and the train was slow. We met many new friends on the way and made the best of things as we worked our way closer to home.

There were no sanitary facilities aboard the train. Every few hours the train would stop and allow the men to go into the woods and relieve themselves. I remember vividly some of the men who had to run after the train with their pants down around their ankles. We helped them on to the moving. I have often wondered what would happen if these men had missed the train and were stranded somewhere in Belgium or France. What would they do?

One of the men in my railroad car had picked up a dog somewhere in Germany, and he became so attached to it that he decided to take him home. He was a Cocker Spaniel. We had a great time watching this dog chasing the light from a flashlight and going around in a circle chasing his tail. The guys on the train made this tedious trip less boring. We were all going home. We were the lucky ones. There were so many thousands of our fellow soldiers who would never make it home to their loved ones, their families, their wives, children, and parents. How is it that we don't realize how fate had spared us and shielded us through the inferno of 1944 and 1945.

At last, the long railroad trip was over and we were herded into the tent camp that was to be our home until the ship that was to take us home arrived in port. I had a difficult time while we were waiting because the food that we had on the train was causing me a problem. We didn't have enough water and I had a case of constipation that had me doubling up in pain. I got through it with difficulty. I threw out half of the stuff in my duffel bag. It was so heavy that I could hardly carry it. We were finally told that on December 3, 1945, my 21st birthday, we would be boarding a liberty ship similar to the one that had been my home for ten days on the way over to England on New Year's Day 1944.

A Sad Farewell

The comedian said, "I've been waiting so long for my ship to come in that the pier collapsed." Well, the ship for thousands of men had come in. It was my birthday. I was twenty-one, and for a guy who never had a birthday party or received any birthday gifts, this was a thrill. We were all ready to go home. It took a couple of hours for us to lug all our gear up the gangway and get settled in to our quarters. We slept in hammocks below deck.

My buddy Jerry was having a difficult time getting his dog on the ship. He was too big to hide in his coat, and the Navy ship didn't allow dogs to be brought aboard. But when Jerry climbed up the gangway he was told that the dog had to go. We were lined up on deck at the railing, and watched as the dog ran up the gangway three times, only to be sent down to the dock each time.

What should have been a happy day in our lives turned out to be sad. As our ship pulled out of the harbor, there, all alone was our Cocker Spaniel. We all had grown to love him. He was sitting on the pier and he grew smaller and smaller until we couldn't see him anymore. It was truly a sad farewell.

Epilogue

Historians will argue about the emergence of the United States as a financial powerhouse. There is no question that when the Japanese attacked Pearl Harbor on December 7, 1941, they awakened a sleeping giant.

The country was so unprepared for war, our soldiers were training with wooden rifles! But the United States responded with alacrity. Our manufacturing muscle started turning out tanks, planes, guns, and millions of men and women were volunteering and being drafted into the service. We were united as one. Our goal was stated by our leader, Franklin Delano Roosevelt.

"We will win through to the inevitable victory, so help us God." Our goal was the unconditional surrender of our enemy.

We were leaving Europe, our job there was done. But victory over Japan was still in doubt. As it turned out, President Harry Truman had to drop two atomic bombs on Nagasaki and Hiroshima before the Japanese surrendered.

When I drove my ambulance onto Omaha Beach in Normandy, and saw the mountains of supplies and equipment, I knew it would only be a matter of time before we defeated the enemy.

It took less than one year. But the sixteen million men who stormed the beaches of France suffered tens of thousands of casualties. I was one of the many wounded who were evacuated to England and then returned to the continent to continue the fight.

It is all now part of the history of the 20th Century. World War II has been called, "The War to end all Wars." The truth is that man has never learned that nobody wins. Man's ultimate folly continues, as Korea, Vietnam, Iraq, and Afghanistan have proved.

I am on my way home. I am young (21) and have my whole life ahead of me. The success a man achieves is strictly up to him. But America is still a place where you can be all that you can be. Of course, a little bit of good luck would help.

Printed in Poland
by Amazon Fulfillment
Poland Sp. z o.o., Wrocław